Other books by Richard and/or Linda Eyre:

LifeBalance
Teaching Children Joy
Teaching Children Responsibility
Teaching Children Sensitivity
Simplified Husbandship/Simplified Fathership
The Awakening (A Novel)
A Joyful Mother of Children
Free to Be Free
I Didn't Plan to Be a Witch
Serendipity of the Spirit
Stewardship of the Heart

# Teaching Your Children Values

## Linda & Richard Eyre

A Fireside Book
Published by Simon & Schuster

New York  London  Toronto
Sydney  Tokyo  Singapore

FIRESIDE

Rockefeller Center
1230 Avenue of the Americas
New York, New York 10020

Copyright © 1993 R. M. Eyre & Associates,
Inc.

DESIGNED BY BARBARA MARKS
Manufactured in the United States of America

20  19  18  17  16  15  14  13

Library of Congress Cataloging-in-Publication
Data

Eyre, Richard.
    Teaching your children values / Richard &
Linda Eyre.
       p.    cm.
    "A Fireside book."
    1. Social values—Study and teaching—
United States.  I. Eyre, Linda.  II. Title.
HM216.E94    1993
649'.1—dc20                92-39038
                            CIP

ISBN: 0-671-76966-9

# Contents

**Introduction: Why? When? Where? Who? What? and How?**  *19*

### Why?

Living by certain tried-and-proven standards is the best route to personal happiness as well as to a stable and productive society.

### When?

Values should be taught to children of all ages—with differing agendas and changing emphasis as children mature.

### Where?

Values are best taught in the home.

### Who?

Parents are the crucial exemplars and instructors.

### What?

Each parent must decide which values to teach. This book is a menu from which to choose and a teaching system that will help with whatever values parents select.

# Contents

*How?*
There are some methods especially well suited to teaching values to preschoolers. Other methods work best for elementary ages, and still others are effective for adolescents.

## VALUES OF BEING

. . . with other individuals, with institutions, with society, with self . . . the inner strength and confidence that is bred by exacting truthfulness, trustworthiness, and integrity

. . . daring to attempt difficult things that are good . . . strength *not* to follow the crowd, to say *no* and mean it and influence others by it . . . being true to convictions and following good impulses, even when they are unpopular or inconvenient . . . boldness to be outgoing and friendly

. . . calmness, peacefulness, serenity . . . the tendency to try to accommodate rather than argue . . . the understanding that differences are seldom resolved through conflict and that meanness in others is an indication of *their* problem or insecurity and thus of their need for your understanding . . . the ability to understand how others feel rather than simply reacting to them . . . control of temper

# Contents

# Contents

# Preface

One morning, while we were living in England, just about the time I began writing this book, I attended an assembly at the "public school" in Surrey where four of our children were students. A public school in Britain is actually a Church of England school, and the assembly that morning had to do with tolerance, individuality, honesty, and the fact that things are not always as they seem. Prayer and hymns were included in the assembly as they were every day in class. After the closing prayer the headmistress invited us all back the next week for the special Easter assembly.

The Church of England is not a strong force in terms of the numbers or ratios of people who attend church on Sunday, but it is the moral force that permeates every institution, from the smallest school to the Houses of Parliament, reminding all Britons of their values and of their morality.

I remember that I returned home from the school assembly that morning and found on our porch my copy of *USA Today,* the newspaper that I got once a week to catch up on the kind of American news and sports that I couldn't find in British newspapers. After I checked the basketball scores and the stock market, I turned to the editorial page, which just happened to be headed, THE DEBATE: VALUES IN SCHOOL.

On one side of the issue Ronald Reagan was quoted: "We don't expect children to discover the principles of calculus on their own, but some would give them no guidance when it comes to ethics, morality and values." And columnist William Raspberry added, "In our zeal to get religion out of the classroom, we threw out morality as well."

On the other side of the issue, an assistance school superintendent from Darien, Connecticut, was quoted: "It's outside the scope of our charge to teach morals. Whose version of ethics would we use?" Also quoted was a somewhat frightening passage from something called *Today's Teen,* a home economics textbook: "Too strict a conscience may make you feel different and unpopular. None of these feelings belong to a healthy personality."

There were other articles, including one about a high school class that was asked if it was right or wrong behavior to return a purse that had been found containing $1,000 to its rightful owner. A majority of students said returning it was foolish behavior. Still another article took the view that public schools can't teach anything adequately and therefore certainly couldn't handle something as complex as values. Also featured was a cartoon of young George Washington, who had just cut down a cherry tree and was saying to his father, "Dad, my teacher says I cannot tell a lie, I cannot tell the truth, and I cannot tell the difference."

I set the paper aside that morning and pondered the different premise that prevails in England or other countries where religion and government are linked rather than separated. On the one hand, I found myself feeling grateful for America's separation of church and state. In a country as diverse and varied as ours, such separation is a necessity. But on the other hand, I found myself agreeing with Raspberry that the prohibition against teaching religion may also prohibit the teaching of values.

Particularly I found myself feeling excited and happy about the book Linda and I had just begun to write (this book, the book you now hold in your hands). I felt very deeply that morning the need for this book, because I realized that even in England or other countries where schools overtly try to teach both values and religion, morality is not truly learned by children unless it is taught in their homes, by the examples and by the conscious efforts of their parents.  —**Richard**

You would not have picked this book up, or bought it, or been drawn to it if you were not interested in values, or if you did not feel the need for some form of value system—particularly in the raising of your children. Thus, we have a great deal in common—a shared interest in values, a shared concern in the raising of our children. We also share the basic goal of helping our children develop a strong character, which can help them to resist the powerful negative influences of some of their peers and of some parts of our culture and society. To parents no goal is more important!

This is not a religious book—any more than "honesty" or "courage" are exclusively religious terms. This is a book that attempts to help parents clarify their own value system and to select basic values to teach to their children. Because values are personal, this is a very personal book: personal stories and incidents are included throughout. In these, and through the ideas and suggestions we make, we present the value system we try to teach to our own family—and teaching *methods* that seem to *work*.

Your value system may be very similar to—or it may differ from—ours. The important thing, we feel, is that parents consciously develop their own set of family values and work at teaching those values to their children. The home will never—should never—*can* never be replaced as the institution where basic values are learned and taught.

Children may grow up and ultimately develop values different from yours and different from what you tried to teach them; but at least they will do so consciously, and with a basis of comparison—with a foundation to start from. If children start from a values vacuum—with none taught, none learned—they will float at the mercy of circumstance and situation, and their lives will never be their own.

Other institutions—schools, churches, scouting, and so forth, may be instrumental in teaching values and morality, but the debate about how, where, and what values should be taught by society is not the issue of this book. At issue here is what is taught within the walls of our homes.

The problem is clarifying (in our own minds) exactly what values we want to teach our children and then finding methods and techniques that actually work in conveying those values (and their desirability) to our children.

This is a book of objectives and a book of methods. It presents twelve specific values that we think most parents can agree on. It suggests that you concentrate on one value each month over the course of one year. And it presents methods that we know can work in teaching each value.

A few important notes about our approach: We have tried hard in this volume to avoid the use of religious words that mean different things to different people and might narrow the number of parents who would feel comfortable using this book.

Our goal has been to deal with values on which virtually all can agree—values that bring people together rather than polarizing or driving them apart—values that, while they may seem deeply religious to some of us and purely practical to others, can nonetheless be agreed upon and saluted by all.

Still, even in our caution, there are some words we could not write without. Just to be certain that you're clear on what we mean, please read on, keeping the following definitions in mind:

By *values* we mean the standards of our actions and the attitudes of our hearts and minds that shape who we are, how we live, and how we treat other people. Good values, of course, shape better people, better lives, and better treatment of others.

By *morality* we mean behavior that is inherently right and that helps rather than hurts other people.

By *traditional* we simply mean time-tested! Old, but not old-fashioned; proven, but not parochial.

The methods in this book are tried and tested. In addition to the considerable laboratory of our own home, they have been used and developed by members of *HOMEBASE,* an international organization of parents who use programs designed around "parenting by objective" to teach their children joy, responsibility, sensitivity, and values (see Postscript).

We hope they will work as well for a Hindu parent in San Francisco as for an Anglican vicar in England . . . as well for an agnostic father from New York as for a Christian mother from Texas or a Jewish parent from Florida.

Our most important hope is that they will work for *you.*

---

*What do we owe a child?*
*Sustenance and shelter . . . roof and raiment.*
*What else?*
*A chance! The best chance we can give to begin and to become.*
*A chance to get past rock and reef into the channel and*
*direction and control to survive the current.*

*What children need is a set of carefully crafted,*
*somewhat magical touchstones*
*which, in youth, transform into moorings,*
*giving first the security of place*
*and then giving growing vessels*
*a chance to be built strong in still water.*

*Later the touchstones transform again—*
*into paddle, rudder, and stern,*
*allowing fresh, new pilots to negotiate and navigate*
*the incredible currents of adult life.*

*The magic touchstones that children need,*
*and that parents owe,*
*are values—*
*values that hold us, secure us, guide us.*

*"But," come the echoes of folly and abdication,*
*"We shouldn't impose our values on children . . . and anyway,*
*people can only learn by experience, by trial and error,*
*each person must discover his own values."*

*As foolish this, as to say, "Calculus must be rediscovered*
*independently by each."*
*True that experience is the teacher,*
*but it can be the experience of parents, and of the ages.*

*Forcing a child to rediscover the wheel of values*
*is withholding a lifeline*
*to a craft stripped of rudder and stern,*
*drastically increasing the chance of drowning.*

————

As we finish this book, we are back in the U.S., a country that is now both fascinated with and divided by the question of "family values."

Forget about the silly, self-serving political debate on "what is a family and what are family values?" Parents already know! Here are twelve specific values that most parents used to teach their children. And the toughest question is not *what,* but *how*.

Linda and Richard Eyre,
Jackson Hole, Wyoming

# Why? When? Where? Who? What? and How?

Before we start to talk about *methods,* let's spend a few moments on *philosophy. Why* we should teach values to children may seem self-evident—but maybe not! *When* values should be taught may be obvious—but maybe you have some questions about when to start. *Who* should teach them and *where* are questions that we may need to reexamine. And we should take a close look at *what* values we should teach and *how* to teach them, since these two questions make up the content and purpose of the rest of this book.

Let's take a quick look at these six questions before we get to implementation.

## WHY?

*Why teach moral values to children?*

Because our parents tried to teach them to us?

Because they are traditional?

Because they are what makes our society safe and workable?

Because we believe in them?

Because they are right?

Because studies show that morality and value-oriented behavior helps a child develop a sense of autonomy, independence, and confidence?

Perhaps all of these are good answers. Certainly at least some of them are correct for each of us.

But there is a better reason . . . a universal one . . . a reason that undergrids and overarches all the rest.

We should teach values to our children because it is the most significant and effective thing we can do for their *happiness.*

The wisdom of the ages—as well as of our own experience—teaches us that individual and collective happiness is connected to (if not the direct product of) behavior that is governed by *moral values*. It is no coincidence that the sages and seers of different cultures and countries have taught the same basic values. The historical correlation between amorality and the decline of Rome corresponds to the personal connections we've all observed in people who seem to lose their principles and their peace of mind at the same time.

One way that our children could learn this connection between living according to values and their personal happiness is by trial and error. The failure and unhappiness that immoral behavior brings could cause them to change, teaching morality and developing values through the hard school of painful experience. But any one person's lifetime is not long enough to "rediscover the wheel"—to sort out all of the connections between values and happiness. Therefore our duty as parents is to pass along what we've learned—to teach our children both the values and the connections.

Ralph Waldo Emerson said it best:

Cause and effect are two sides of one fact. Every secret is told, every crime is punished, every virtue is rewarded, every wrong is redressed, in silence and certainty . . . cause and effect, means and ends, seed and fruit, cannot be severed; for the effect already blooms in the cause, the end pre-exists in the means, the fruit is in the seed.

The fruit of fulfillment and basic happiness is in the seed of clear, strong moral values.

So . . . why teach values to our children?

*Because their happiness depends on it!*

## WHEN?

The "permissive parenting" of the sixties has produced a generation of young adults who have broken all records for drug abuse, family instability, suicide, and (though it is less quantifiable) unhappiness.

One of the tenets of permissive (also known as "liberal" or "democratic" or "freedom-emphasizing") parenting is the idea of avoiding the teaching of moral values until children are "old enough to choose their own value system."

This approach is a catastrophic mistake.

It is analogous to setting a tiny, powerless vessel down in the midst of turbulent, destructive currents and hoping that by some chance it will wash into a safe harbor.

With or without their parents' help, children will begin developing both conscious and subconscious values during their preschool years. They learn them partly from their friends, partly from television, but mostly from their family. They test and develop and sometimes alter these values as they enter school. As they approach adolescence, they struggle for autonomy and begin to set up their own value system, which is independent of (but not usually very different from) that of their parents.

If their parents avoid educating them regarding values, they'll learn—primarily—that values aren't important. The personal-value-developing process works better when parents focus on values and consciously try to help, teach, and set examples all along the way. Their children will still develop their own values—but they will do so *because* their parents showed them that it was an important part of their development.

This book presents a positive program for parents— a proactive approach that we call parenting by objective rather than a defensive strategy of reacting to our children. *Teaching Your Children Values* provides ideas and methods that can assist parents in focusing on one clear objective *each month*. In this book each of the twelve "months," or chapters, will concentrate on the how-tos for one specific and particular *value*. Parents, focusing on a separate value each month, will find themselves teaching it to children in all kinds of ways, both consciously and subconsciously.

Each of the twelve "months" opens with a personal incident or story illustrating the value to be focused on and then explains methods for teaching that particular value to preschoolers. These preschool methods always revolve around simple stories, demonstrations, and little poems or songs that help small children grasp the *nature* of that value and feel the *desirability* of it. They also include methods of praise and reinforcement for value-reflecting behavior.

Next in each chapter come methods for elementary-age children. Here the emphasis is on the kind of games, awards, memorizing, and more elaborate stories that are so effective with six- to twelve-year-olds.

Each "month" ends with a third set of more advanced methods for young adolescents. Here we rely more on discussion, role-playing, and opinion-and-experience sharing.

The answer to the question of *when* we should teach moral values to our children is at every age. The answer is:

*NOW*
and
*ALWAYS*.

## WHERE?

The debate that rages around us about whether morality should be taught in schools is interesting, but in some ways irrelevant.

The reason it is somewhat irrelevant is that what is

taught in the home, in either the positive or the negative sense, can be far more influential on children than what is taught in school or in any other institution.

For one thing parents have at least a five-year head start on public schools. For another thing parents have the potential to be, during at least the first fourteen or fifteen years of life, a drastically more influential force (both by example and by concept) on their children than any other person, factor, element, or group.

It *is* so and it *ought* to be so. The family is the basic institution. Parents have the basic responsibility. And the basic joy that results from conscientious effort to teach children correct moral values is deep and lasting (as well as contagious and transferable).

Where?

In the family!

In the home!

## WHO?

Some parents, well meaning and with undeniable love for their children, still make the mistake of taking the "general contractor" approach to parenting. Just as the general contractor creates houses by "jobbing out" the actual building to the carpenter, the plumber, the electrician, the mason, many parents expect the "subcontractors" of schoolteachers, scout leaders, ministers, summer-camp staff, music instructors, and counselors to build the morality and value systems of their children.

And it doesn't work very well!

These subcontractors and the institutions and organizations they represent can supplement, support, and back up the parent—but to ask or expect them to do more than that constitutes a default both of responsibility and of fulfillment.

Who?

Parents?

Who?

You!

## WHAT?

Are there such things as universal values? Is there such a thing as unconditional, unchanging, nondenominational morality? Are there certain standards of thought and behavior that are inherently right and that can be unequivocally accepted as good, or at least as "better" than their opposites or alternatives?

We have wrestled with these questions—not as philosophers trying to create a universal value system but as *parents* who want to be clear about what matters to us and about what we hope matters to our children. As writers we have grappled with defining the word *values,* with separating values from mere attributes or skills, and with sorting out a list of inclusive values that other parents can agree with, understand, embrace, and teach.

It has been anything but easy. We have struggled to develop a *definition,* a set of *criteria,* and a *list,* and we are neither naive enough nor pretentious enough to think that our list will work perfectly for everyone else. Indeed, values *must be* personal, and let us emphasize again that the goal of this book is not to "convert" the reader to any particular value but to help parents know how to teach their children the values they choose to teach.

Think with us through our definition, our criteria, and our list—and use the opportunity to reassess your own values and your own thoughts about values. Remember, as you do, that the objective is neither to judge yourself nor to justify yourself. Think in terms of what you now believe to be good values and in terms of what values you feel will enhance and bring joy to the lives of your children. There may very well be values that you did not hold or standards you did not keep that you nonetheless hope to see more fully developed and practiced in the lives of your children. There is no inconsistency in this, and certainly no hypocrisy. We all hope to teach better than we learned. We all want our children to surpass us. Indeed we want our children to learn from *our* experience, both from what we feel we've done well and from what we now might do differently.

---

Early in the process of writing this book we showed an outline to a friend of mine, one who came from a difficult childhood in a broken home, who had tried all kinds of lifestyles and only recently settled down and started her own family. She read through the twelve values we had listed, together with our brief definition/explanation of each. Then she closed the manuscript, slapped her hand down on it, and said, "Well, I agree. I'd like to teach all of these values to my children, but I'm afraid I'd feel a little hypocritical on some of them!"

I guess I looked a little puzzled, because she elaborated.

"After all, you can't expect them to do something you didn't do or be something you never were, can you?"

I still didn't say anything. I was thinking about what she'd just said. She was thinking about it, too, and realizing that it didn't make much sense. She went on, looking for words that would justify the position she'd just taken.

"Well, I mean, you can't very well say, 'Do as I say, not as I did,' can you?"

I waited. Her own thought process had too much momentum to interrupt, and the momentum turned her right around.

"That's silly, isn't it? I guess if I believe something is good, or right, or at least *better,* I should want it for my children. Maybe they don't have to duplicate my experience to decide what I've decided." **—Linda**

First, a *definition:*

*A true and universally acceptable "value" is one that produces behavior that is beneficial both to the practitioner and to those on whom it is practiced.* It is a principle that either accomplishes well-being or prevents harm (or does both). It is something that *helps* or something that prevents *hurt.*

Each of the twelve values briefly described in the table of contents (and further elaborated on in the chapters that follow) meets this definition.

Next, a *criterion:*

For our purposes as parents and for our clarification as writers, we apply to the term *values* further criteria that separate them from various skills, attributes, or characteristics that may also be beneficial. The differentiation is this: A *value* is a quality distinguished by: (a) its ability to multiply and increase in our possession even as it is given away; and (b) the fact (even the *law*) that the more it is given to others, the more it will be returned by others and received by ourselves.

To illustrate: Honesty is *defined* as a value because it *benefits* both the practitioner and the persons on whom it is practiced. So is love, so is kindness, so is justice, and so on. These qualities also pass the *criteria* for values because even as we give them, we have more of them left, and because the more of them we give, the more of them will come back into our lives from others.

For our purposes, then, personality traits such as ambition, mathematical genius, physical beauty, wealth, or goal-setting ability, while they may be positive characteristics, useful skills, fortunate circumstances, or pleasing traits, *are not universal values*. Ambition and goals benefit only the individual—they do not always benefit those they are perpetrated on. Wealth does not increase as it is given away. Physical beauty or mathematical genius, even if they could be given, would not necessarily be given back.

Values, then, are other-and-self-benefiting qualities that are given as they are gained and gained as they are given.

Now, a *list:* Have another look through the twelve values listed and briefly defined in the table of contents. See if you think they fit the definition and the criteria. More importantly, see if they fit your feelings about what you want to give and teach to your children.

So much of life, in today's world, has to do with *getting*. Values, in contrast, have to do with *being* and with *giving*. It is who we are and what we give rather than what we have that makes up our truest inner selves. And it is what we are and what we give of ourselves to our children that will, more than any other force or factor, determine what their values are and influence who they will be and what they will give.

Of the twelve values we have selected, half have been called *values of being* because they begin with the development of a quality or an attitude within ourselves that determines how we behave and how we treat others. The other half are called *values of giving* because they originate as gifts to others and then go on to influence who we are.

But do not carry the distinction of the two categories too far. They meet, overlap, and blend. The *values of being* (honesty, courage, peaceability, self-reliance, discipline, and fidelity) are given as they are gained—practiced on the "outer" as they are developed in the "inner." And the *values of giving* (respect, love, loyalty, unselfishness, kindness, and mercy) are gained as they are given and developed as they are practiced.

The purpose of the distinction and the division is only to fix a starting point. We start to develop discipline or self-reliance or peaceability by practicing it on ourselves and within ourselves. We start to develop love or sensitivity or mercy by practicing it on (and giving it to) others. But the giving and receiving, the growing and contributing, quickly blur and merge. We soon practice love and respect on ourselves and build it within us; and we soon give discipline or peaceability to others through our commitment and example.

A diagram can help show the starting points and the flow:

*Values of Being*
(who we are)

*Values of Giving*
(what we give)

Honesty ⟶
Courage ⟶
Peaceability ⟶
Self-reliance, Potential ⟶
Discipline, Moderation ⟶
Fidelity, Chastity ⟶

⟵ Loyalty, Dependability
⟵ Respect
⟵ Love
⟵ Unselfishness, Sensitivity
⟵ Kindness, Friendliness
⟵ Justice, Mercy

Each value *starts* in an attitude of being or an action of giving, then becomes an action as well as an attitude— or, a quality as well as a gift. And then the gaining and the giving feed and build on each other, each catalyzing and energizing and nurturing the other.

One secret that the diagram reveals is that the two great *methods* for teaching all twelve values are *being* and *giving*.

Being and giving are not only the test of our values but the means by which we teach and transmit them to others, particularly to our children.

A final word on the question of *what:* Many look at the list of twelve values and say, "But where is wisdom? or where is humor? or where is self-esteem? or where is autonomy? or where is faith? or where is caution or a healthy wariness?" Whatever you see missing from the list can be found in one of two places:

**a.** Hidden *in* the list of twelve. As you read the chapters, you will see that the twelve values are broader than their titles.

**b.** In your own head. If there are other values you want to teach that you don't find here—*teach* them. The methods or ideas for values you do find here will help.

Do not feel bound by the sequence in which these twelve values appear in the book. Each is independent and can be taken up first, last, or in between. The important thing is that you pick out *one* to focus on *every* month. At the beginning of each month select the value that seems most relevant or most applicable or most *needed* by you and your children at the moment and during the month ahead.

So . . . the answer to the question *what:*

*The twelve universal values . . . added to or subtracted*

*from or modified by your own list, your own desires, your own hopes for your own children.*

## HOW?

As just mentioned, the supreme *methods* for teaching values to children are the examples of our own *being* and our own *giving*.

Example is always the best teacher—and what we *do* always overwhelms and overshadows and outteaches what we *say*.

———

A friend of ours told us of a day when she got so upset with two small preschoolers fighting over a doll that she grabbed the doll and threw it out the window. She then lectured the little children on sharing and on not fighting and was sure when she had finished that she had taught them something.

She had! Later that day she found the children throwing loaves of bread out the window. Children will always learn more from what they see us do than from what they hear us say! **—Linda**

———

While example is the prime teacher, close behind (and closely interrelated) are the methods of storytelling, games, role-playing, and imagination.

This book includes a host of methods, because it is difficult for most of us to think of our own stories, our own games. Remember, though, that some of the best methods are the ones we do think of on the spur of the moment, when the need arises. And one thing that helps us think is to have a clear goal. We all think better when we have a purpose . . . like the specific objective of

teaching one separate and individual value to our children each month. Thus the rest of this book is not in
chapters but in "months." Focus on one value at a time,
one for each month of the year. When you finish the
series of twelve, start over again—your children will be
a year older the next time through and will be ready to
learn each value at a different level.

When we adopt a specific goal each month—a particular value that we want to concentrate on and teach—
and when we are given a selection of methods from
which to choose, we can answer the question of "how."

There are certain methods and techniques that are
particularly well suited to teaching moral values. Let's
become generally acquainted with them now, because
they are used frequently in the "months" that follow.

- *"Scenarios" and various kinds of verbal games* are helpful because they allow children to actually put
  themselves in situations and "see" the consequences and the cause-and-effect ramifications of
  various choices or behavior.
- *Concept discussions,* where children talk about the
  terms and concepts of morality (on their own level)
  with parents helping them develop both their
  own interest and their own ability to "really talk"
  with a grown-up. Studies have shown that there
  are direct relationships between the moral behavior of children and the amount of time spent just
  talking with parents. Our own values are steadily
  and gradually communicated to children as we
  interact.
- *Praise with reinforcement* is the one method with the
  power to turn moral behavior into consistent, con-

scious habit. The duke of Wellington, near the end of his life, was asked what one thing he would change if he could live his life over again. "I would give more praise" was his reply. Pointing out failure doesn't change things—it produces guilt and perpetuates the status quo. Real change comes through catching children doing something good and then praising and reinforcing the behavior.

---

One Sunday afternoon I looked up over the newspaper I was reading and noticed a rather distraught, unhappy look on the face of six-year-old Jonah.

"What's wrong, buddy?"

"Oh, nothing."

"You sure?"

"Yeah."

I looked back to the newspaper, but my mind wasn't on the words. I was thinking of yesterday afternoon—the soccer game—and the miserable little kid who had called Jonah a "klutz."

I put down the paper and pulled Jo up on my knee.

"You know, buddy, I've been thinking a lot lately about some things you are extra good at."

"Me?"

"Yes. Do you know that you're incredibly good at being friendly to other kids?"

I went on telling him things I thought he was extra good at. The list included "making the baby laugh," "saying your r's clearly," and "remembering to brush your teeth." Jonah's whole demeanor changed before my eyes. His posture changed, his expression changed to a glow. His eyes took on a sparkle. He soaked up the praise like a dry sponge.

"Dad, let's write these down!"

"Write what down?"

"Write down these things I'm good at!" He wanted to preserve them, to lay claim to them.

"Where?" I said, glancing around for a piece of paper.

Jonah looked around, too, but saw nothing appropriate there in the living room to write on.

"Here," he said, "right here on my hand. Write with your pen on my hand the things that I'm good at."

And I did. And he didn't wash his hand until his mom made him.

—Richard

--------

- *Reward, awards* and any other form of recognition coupled with praise is a powerful way of promoting moral behavior. In addition to various types of rewards, specific *awards* (plaques that recognize special effort at a particular value during a given week) can be both a lively discussion point and a motivating compliment.
- *"Second chance"* and *"let's start over"* approaches by parents can correct behavior and remind children of moral values without the negative effects of punishment and criticism.
- *Memorization* of short, graphic phrases or mottoes that state a particular value in a clever and memorable way is valuable in planting a good concept firmly in children's minds.
- *The value and its opposite: Which helps, which hurts?* By guiding children to discover antonyms of each value, you can set up "opposite poles" and put yourself in a position to ask which one hurts people and which one helps people.
- *Acknowledgment of positive behavior, ignoring of negative behavior.* Children crave attention, and all too often parents give attention to negative behavior

and ignore positive behavior. We tend to "leave well enough alone" and spend all our effort correcting what is wrong. We need to turn this around and, again, "catch them doing something right."

---

While living in Japan I saw a wonderfully perfect example of something we all know we should do as parents—namely giving our attention to positive rather than negative behavior (something parents in Eastern countries seem better at than most Western parents).

I had gone next door to borrow a book. The Japanese neighbor lady let me in, and as we were chatting, her little boy began to fuss and cry and impatiently pull on her skirt. She completely ignored him and continued to focus all her attention on me. The little fellow got louder and more insistent, and the mother just scooped him up—while still talking to me—and simply opened the nearest door, put him down on the other side of it and closed the door. It happened to be a closet. In a few moments the child came out and very politely asked for what he wanted. This time the mother responded.

When we went upstairs to find the book, we discovered that her two other children were sitting quietly, playing together. Now she interrupted our conversation to go over and compliment the children for their behavior.

The recognition, praising, and rewarding of positive behavior and the ignoring of negative behavior—I had just witnessed a perfect example!   **—Richard**

---

Each value (each month) includes a separate set of suggested methods for preschool, elementary, and young adolescent ages. You will focus, of course, during each month, on the methods specified and appropriate for your child's age (or children's ages).

With preschoolers the most effective methods are simple games, stories, and a great deal of praise and reinforcement.

With elementary ages awards are particularly effective, as are memorizing, consequence games, and other verbal games that require more thought.

With young adolescents "adult discussions," "help and hurt" dialogues, and case studies of other teenagers draw the highest interest.

These methods, separately applied for each particular value and combined with our own individual ideas, become the tools in parents' hands and the know-how that can make us all into confident "values-teachers."

———

When we began our somewhat organized effort to teach the values in this book to our own children, we started with a family meeting—kind of a kickoff to explain what we were going to try to teach and *why.*

As with most family meetings this one turned out to be a mixed bag. There were some short attention spans and a lot of "when will this be over?" and "I need to go and call my friend now."

But we all learned some things, and we set the stage for the "months" ahead. We explained what *values* means and went through the list of twelve. We told the children as directly and convincingly as we could that the *reason* we wanted them to learn values was because we deeply believed that values were the things that make people happy. We also introduced the word *morality* as something that described doing the "right" thing and following our values. We even quoted Ernest Hemingway, who said, "Moral is what you feel good after. Immoral is what you feel bad after."   —**Linda**

———

So . . . how?
*With the methods that come from this book.*
*And with the methods that come from your own mind as*

*you tune in to your children and to the goal of teaching one particular value each month.*

(Note: Each chapter will include an "award" for those who do well at the month's value. We've found this a particularly effective way of involving children in learning values.)

# Values

## of Being

# Honesty

*Honesty with other individuals, with institutions, with society, with self. The inner strength and confidence that is bred by exacting truthfulness, trustworthiness, and integrity.*

———

Pulling into the driveway one day, I noticed a broken milk bottle on the pavement. I asked nine-year-old Josh and his friend, Chip, if they knew how it happened. Chip quickly said no. Josh looked over at him, somewhat startled, then walked over and put his hand on Chip's shoulder and said, "It's okay, he'll understand." Then to me, "The basketball hit it, Dad. Sorry. We were going to clean it up, but we forgot. Come on, Chip, I'll get the dustpan."

I listened through the window as they were sweeping up. "One thing I've learned," Josh was counseling Chip, a full six months his junior, "is that you get in a lot less trouble when you just go ahead and tell the truth." **—Richard**

Teaching children honesty can be a real challenge, given the examples of dishonesty that they will encounter every day in the world around them. Your example, and your constant feedback about your child's behavior, can be a powerful influence on your child. Along with your example, we have discovered some other teaching methods that work. These methods are presented (as they are in each chapter) in four brief sections. First, general guidelines for children of all ages; then methods aimed at preschoolers, elementary-age children, and adolescents.

## GENERAL GUIDELINES

*Be completely honest with your children.* This will show them how always applicable the principle is and will demonstrate your commitment to it. Answer their questions truthfully and candidly unless it is a question that is off-limits, and then tell them simply and honestly why you won't answer it. Never let them hear you tell little "convenient lies" on the phone and never ask them to tell one for you ("My mommy isn't home"). Don't exaggerate. Don't threaten to do things you don't really intend to do.

*Give praise and the chance to "start over."* This gives children a quick second chance to be truthful. Don't be anxious to "catch" your children in a lie. Instead "catch them telling the truth" and praise them for it. If they do tell (or begin to tell) what you think is an untruth, interrupt and say, "Wait, think for a minute. Remember that it's important to tell the truth." Then let them start over.

*Point out consequences.* Show your children the cause-and-effect dynamics of honesty and dishonesty. Watch for situations (in real life, on TV, etc.) where a dishonest act was performed. Point out the consequences to both the object of the act (the person or institution that was cheated or hurt or deceived) and the doer of the act. Also look for illustrations of honesty and mention the positive consequences, especially the inner peace, confidence, and self-respect gained by the honest individual.

## Methods for Preschoolers

### The Demonstration Game

This game can help small children grasp the concept and know the terminology.

Ask, "Do you know the difference between something that's true and something that's not true? Let's see if you do. I'll say something and you say, 'True' or 'Not true.'" Start with simple physical facts and move toward things relating to behavior, for example:

- The sky is green. (Kids say, "Not true.")
- (Point at foot) This is my foot. (Kids say, "True.")
- Ants are bigger than elephants.
- We see with our eyes.
- We hear with our nose.
- Milk comes from chickens.
- Take a cookie out of a jar and eat it. Then say, "I didn't eat the cookie."
- Drop a toy on the couch. Then say, "Yes, I left my toy on the couch."

Then say, "You really *can* tell the difference between true and not true, can't you? Do you know what it's called when someone says something that's not true? It's called a *lie*."

Now: "I'll say some more things and you say, 'Truth' if it's true and 'Lie' if it's not true."

- Pick up a dollar on the floor. Then say, "I didn't find a dollar."
- Give a bit of food to someone else. Then say, "No, I didn't eat all my food. I gave some of it to————."

(Use illustrations appropriate to your child or children.)

Then ask, "Why is telling the truth better than telling a lie?" (So that everyone knows what really happened; so the wrong person won't get blamed; so we can learn to do better, etc.)

### Give Effusive, Elaborate Praise

This encourages honesty on a day-to-day basis. Preschoolers will repeat behavior they receive attention for. They prefer positive attention (praise) to negative attention (reproval or punishment), but they prefer negative attention to no attention at all.

Therefore, when small children lie, try to give them as little attention as possible (other than quietly letting them know that you know it's not the truth). When they tell the truth, praise them extravagantly. And when they tell the truth in terms of admitting they did something wrong ("Who wrote on this wall?"), make the praise you give them for telling the truth outweigh the punishment or redress you give them for what they did. Preschoolers can understand the distinction and the separation between your displeasure with what they did and your pleasure with their truthfulness.

---

One interesting development in our family efforts to teach honesty occurred when our twenty-month-old baby, Charity, learned two new words. She already knew how to say the names of each of her eight brothers and sisters (or at least her version of those names). Then one week she learned two new words: *did it*. With those words and her siblings' names she became an instant, expert tattletale. Whenever we asked, "Who made this mess?" or "Who squeezed the toothpaste out?" little Charity, who is a marvelously observant child, would tell us the answer.

One result was that the other children became more thoroughly honest—or at least more *quickly* honest about what they had done. Charity the Enforcer, one of her brothers began to call her.  **—Richard**

## The Honesty-About-Feelings Game

This will help small children realize that feelings are caused by what has happened—and that it is okay to feel things and okay to tell others honestly how we feel. Go through a magazine (one with lots of ads and colored pictures) and point at faces saying, "How do you think he feels?" Then say, "Why do you think he feels that way?" Then say, "Is it okay to feel that way?"

Help children to identify feelings and their probable causes and to know that it's okay to feel those things and to tell other people how they feel.

## Methods for Elementary School Age

### The Consequence Game

This game can help children understand that the long-term consequences of honesty are always better than the long-term consequences of dishonesty.

Prepare pairs of simple index cards or small sheets of paper. On one side of each of the cards in the pair describe two alternative courses of action—one honest and one dishonest—along with the short-term consequences of each action. Fill out the other side of the cards so that when the two cards are flipped over, the long-term consequences are revealed. Play it as a game, letting children decide, by looking at the front sides only, which option they would take.

*Front sides:*

You are at the store buying something and the clerk gives you $10 too much change. You keep it. After all, it was his mistake and not yours. You go into the toy store next door and buy some new handle grips for your bike.

When the clerk gives you the $10 extra change, you tell him he has given you too much and give the $10 back to him. He says thanks, but as you walk out, you start thinking about the new handle grips you could have bought with the $10.

*Reverse sides:*

You know the money wasn't yours. You start to worry that the clerk will have to pay the store $10 out of his wages. Whenever you ride your bike, the new handle grips remind you that you were dishonest.

You feel good and strong inside because you were honest. Whenever you ride your bike, you remember that you need handle grips, but you also remember that you were honest.

*Front sides:*

You are sitting in class taking a really hard test that you forgot to study for. The girl across the aisle seems to know all the answers, and her paper is so easy to see. You copy a few answers and end up getting an A − on the test.

You're a little mad at yourself for not studying harder and you're really worried about your grade. Still, you keep your eyes on your paper and do your best. Unfortunately your best that day is only a C on the test.

*Reverse sides:*

Your conscience bothers you. You know that you didn't deserve the A. You wonder if anyone saw you cheating. It's a little hard for you to get to sleep that night. On the next test you're unprepared again.

You resolve to study harder. Next test you do better. You like yourself because you know you are honest. Other people like you because they know you can be trusted.

Develop other cards to meet your own situation. Let the short-term consequence of a dishonest act be good, the long-term consequence bad. Develop cards on honesty with parents, with siblings, with friends, with institutions, and so on.

After playing the game ask the question What could a person do if he made the dishonest choice and felt bad about it afterward? (He could return the money, apologize, etc.)

### The Honesty Pact

Decide in advance, within your family, to be strictly honest with each other. Toward the end of this "month" on honesty, get together as a family around the dinner table or on an outing. Thank the children for their help in thinking about honesty during the month. Review what everyone has learned. Ask if anyone knows what a "pact" is. Suggest that the family have a pact of strict honesty so that every family member can explicitly trust every other family member. Write up a short pact, starting with the words "We promise each other . . ." Let everyone (parents and children) sign the pact.

### The Honesty-Under-Pressure Award

This is a motivational way to get children to evaluate their personal honesty every week. On Sundays (or whatever day you most often get your whole family together for a meal) ask, "Who had a situation this past week where it was a challenge to be honest?" Have an "award" on hand to give to the person who remembers the best incident of being honest. A piece of construction paper or colored card with a neatly printed H.U.P. (Honesty Under Pressure) will do nicely as the award. Let the child (or adult) who wins put it on his bedroom door during the week until it is awarded again the next week.

After a couple of weeks of "getting used to," you will find that children are willing to think hard about their behavior of the past week in hopes of winning the award. And it is this kind of thinking and recognition that strongly reinforces honesty.

**Story: "Isabel's Little Lie"**

Tell the following story to help your children understand how one lie can lead to another and produce serious consequences:

One day Isabel told a little lie. She wasn't supposed to feed her dinner to her dog, Barker, but she did, and when her mother came in and saw her plate all clean, Isabel said that she had eaten it all. (That was a little lie, wasn't it?) The dinner was chicken, and Barker got a bone in his throat. Pretty soon he started to cough and snort and act very uncomfortable.

"Do you know what's wrong with Barker?" asked Mother. "No," said Isabel. (That was another lie, wasn't it? But Isabel *had* to do it so that Mother wouldn't know she told the first lie.) Mother looked in Barker's mouth but couldn't see anything. "Did Barker eat something, Isabel?"

"I don't know, Mommy." (That was another lie, wasn't it? But she didn't want her mother to know about the first two lies.)

Barker got worse, and Mother took him to the animal hospital. Isabel went too. "What happened to the dog?" asked the doctor. "We don't know," said Isabel. (That was another lie, wasn't it? But if Isabel had told, then Mother and the dog doctor would know she had lied before.) The dog doctor said, "If it's just a bone, we could get it out with an instrument, but it might be glass, so we may have to operate."

Isabel decided it was time to tell the truth. She said, "It's a bone, and I *did* know Barker ate it, and I *didn't* eat all my dinner, and I *did* give it to Barker, and I won't tell lies anymore, because if you tell one, you might have to tell more and more." Isabel started to cry, but her mother loved her and she decided she really would tell the truth from then on.

(Note: Each chapter will have one or more children's stories illustrating that month's value—written for elementary-age children but adaptable for younger or older children.)

### The Pantomime Game

This game can help children to identify honest emotions—in themselves and in others—and to know that it is okay to feel and to talk about these emotions.

Write each of the following emotion-related adjectives on a small card. Shuffle the cards and give five to each family member. Each player has forty-five seconds to pantomime the actions (gestures, facial expressions, etc.) associated with the word on the card. Score one point for each motion correctly guessed. After each person has a turn, shuffle the cards and distribute five to each person again and repeat the process until one person scores 10 points. Eventually children will learn how to better display the emotions they feel as well as how to recognize them in others. The idea is to help children to accept their own emotions, recognize how others are feeling, and be able to talk honestly about both.

Here is a list of emotions, feelings, and attitudes to pantomime:

| | | | |
|---|---|---|---|
| loving | remorseful | concerned | thoughtful |
| kind | appreciative | trusting | cheerful |
| optimistic | nice | calm | helpful |
| empathetic | affectionate | warm | forgiving |
| grateful | serene | tender | interested |
| loyal | friendly | responsible | gentle |
| sensitive | free | reliable | passive |
| active | respectful | cooperative | hurt |
| sly | untruthful | honorable | jealous |
| mean | unfriendly | foolish | guilty |
| angry | defensive | greedy | annoyed |
| envious | fair | unfair | disgusted |
| selfish | sorry | insensitive | remorseful |
| spoiled | rude | unequal | cowardly |
| resentful | | | |

## Methods for Adolescents

### Analyze Types of Dishonesty

This kind of discussion can help older children to grasp the broader definitions of honesty and dishonesty.

Say, "There are really a lot of different types of dishonesty. Let's see how many we can list." With some encouragement children will list many of the following:

Cheating on tests
Cheating on taxes
Cheating on expense reports

Calling a ball out in a tennis game that you're not
    sure was out
Exaggerating
Telling someone they look nice when they really don't
    (flattery)
Not telling the whole truth so you won't get in
    trouble
Twisting the truth just a little so it won't sound so
    bad
Lying to protect yourself
Lying to protect someone else

Keep the list growing by asking subquestions, such as What are some kinds of dishonesty to parents? What are some kinds of dishonesty to self?

Saying you got in earlier than you really did
Not being able to admit it when you are scared or
    worried or insecure

### Discuss Types of Dishonesty

Follow up on the foregoing discussion of types of dishonesty to help children to want total honesty for themselves. Ask, "Are any of these forms of dishonesty okay? What about white lies or little exaggerations? (Help them to see that even "little lies" are usually unnecessary: You can think a little harder and come up with an honest compliment; you don't really need to exaggerate, etc. If you're going to be honest, why not be completely honest?)

### Opposite Word: Which Helps? Which Hurts?

This activity can help children grasp the *effects* of honesty and of its opposites on other people. Ask your children for antonyms or opposites of dishonesty (go behond *dishonesty* to words like *deceptive* or *lie* or *cheat*, then ask *how* these words hurt and *whom* they can hurt. Ask how honesty helps and whom it can help.

(Note: There is a similar "help or hurt" method in each chapter dealing with that month's value and its opposites).

The acceptance of "white lies" may be one reason that many people discount the whole notion of values. There is a feeling of inner confidence and security that comes with uncompromising honesty, and we should help our children to have that power even if we have not always had it ourselves.

### Share Your Own Honesty Dilemmas

This can help demonstrate to older children that you are willing to be honest with them—even about your own struggles with honesty. Be brave enough to tell your children about times when you have had a hard time being honest. Tell them "positive" incidents when you were honest and negative ones when you weren't— and tell them about any current situations where you are struggling to be completely honest.

This kind of sharing is quite a compliment to your older children because it expresses your confidence in their maturity. Nothing will inspire more trust from them or encourage them more to share *their* struggles with you.

Nothing impresses young adolescents more than drama . . . and the dilemmas that certain kinds of drama can depict. While living in London, we took our twelve- and fourteen-year-old to the marvelous stage musical *Les Misérables,* based on Victor Hugo's great work of fiction. In one scene Jean Valjean, the fugitive and former convict whose life has been changed by the love and generosity of an old priest, learns that another man who resembles him has been apprehended for his crime and is about to go on trial. The other man is a drifter of no consequence, while Jean Valjean has become a wealthy and important man on whom many depend. He sings a song about the agony of his conscience: "If I come forward, I am condemned. If I stay silent, I am damned." Then he does step forward, saving the other man and preserving his own integrity.

After the show I asked the children what they liked best. "The part about the conscience," said our twelve-year-old. "He did what was right. He told the truth, and that's the reason that everything worked out in the end."  **—Richard**

### The Scenario Game

This game will help children think through situations in advance. Define *scenario* as "a projected possibility with consequences." Then define possibility and consequences (appeal to the adolescent desire to use big words and "speak grown-up"). Then, in your own words, expand and elaborate on the following "case studies." The more dramatic and storylike, the better.

*Cheating.* You're sitting in your English class, taking the final exam. You've studied hard, and the first two sections of the test are easy. The last section is much harder, and you realize it is from a book you forgot to review. You're pretty sure the teacher never told you to read that book. You feel mad at the teacher and that it's not your fault that you don't know the answers. The questions are multiple choice, and it's extremely easy to see Jim's answers across the aisle.

*Exaggerating.* Your family has just moved to town. You've started at a new school and made some brand-new friends. In the lunchroom they are asking what you did in sports at your former school. You were actually only a substitute on one team, but they don't know that. You wonder if you should tell them what you wish had happened, instead of what actually did.

*Protecting yourself.* You got in an hour later than your parents had requested. They had fallen asleep, so you didn't disturb them. It's now the morning after, and they ask you what time you came in.

*Think of other scenarios* (or use actual situations that you know of). Help your children (through discussion) arrive at the conclusion (and project it into each case study) that most dishonesty seems to solve a short-term problem or create a short-term benefit but leads to less confidence in self over the long run.

# Courage

*Daring to attempt difficult things that are good. Strength not to follow the crowd, to say no and mean it and influence others by it. Being true to convictions and following good impulses even when they are unpopular or inconvenient. Boldness to be outgoing and friendly.*

———

Eight-year-old Talmadge: "Yeah—it takes real courage to be a chicken."

Dad: "What do you mean by that?"

Talmadge: "Well, I mean, like if kids are trying to get you to do something that you don't think is right—or it's really, really dangerous, and they're saying you're chicken, then it takes real courage to be a chicken and say, Yeah, I'm a chicken.' "

Dad: "Now, why couldn't I have said it like that?"

We had been talking about courage, and I'd been trying, in my long-winded way, to explain the difference between the *true* courage of being a leader for the right, standing up for what you believe, and resisting peer pressure and the *false* courage of accepting dares, taking risks, being foolhardy. I had been trying to communicate the idea that real bravery was an inner thing, closely related to integrity and being true to yourself, and unrelated to the sort of outward bravado and macho chance taking that seems to be the message of so much of our media.

It was there that Talmadge interrupted with, "Yeah, it takes real courage to be a chicken." —**Richard**

———

———

Our family had returned to England for six months with two objectives: first, to get away from interruptions and commitments long enough to finish some writing; second, to get the children into British schools for a couple of terms to broaden their horizons.

After the first four months we were meeting the first objective and doing pretty well on the second—with the exception of ten-year-old Jonah. Fate had dealt him a schoolteacher who went beyond the expected British firmness and discipline and was just plain *mean*. And among the usually polite British children in his class were a couple of boys who picked on him, and a whole group who tried to get him to use bad language. On top of it all, Jonah got a respiratory infection that turned into pneumonia and put him into the hospital. By the time he recovered, there were only two or three weeks of the school year left, and Jonah, quite naturally, could see very little point in going back and a big bunch of reasons for staying home.

We expected that if he didn't go back, he would always view the England experience as a negative one. Yet we didn't want to force him—so we had another family discussion on courage. With lots of help from his older brothers and sisters, we decided that courage meant doing hard things that were *hard* but that were also *right* or *best* in the long run. We talked about the rewards that come from choosing the difficult but right path. We talked about getting right back on a horse that bucks you off. But we tried to understand how he felt, and we left it up to Jonah.

He couldn't quite bring himself to a commitment to go back for the rest of the term, but he finally worked up the spark of courage to say he'd go back to see how bad it was.

At that point we decided it was time to leave as little as possible to chance. We visited privately with his teacher, telling her the situation and asking her to try to give more encouragement and less criticism. I walked to school the first day with Jonah, tried to meet several of his classmates, and talked with them about American football, their favorite subject, hoping that Jonah would feel comfortable continuing the conversation.

And then we praised Jonah. Oh, how we praised him. "What courage, Jonah— what courage to go and do something that *hard!*"

It turned out to be a great experience. He worked *hard* and got some A's those last few weeks. He tried *hard* to follow instructions and got some commendations from his usually critical teacher. And he tried *hard* to have social interaction with classmates, but was strong in refusing to swear or use their bad language. Two or three of them admired him for it, became friends, and later pen pals.

We had tried to help Jonah implement courage, and his situation had helped us to define what the word meant.   **—Linda**

So . . . courage means doing the right thing when it is hard (and even if it means being called a "chicken").

Children can learn what courage is through stories, games, role-playing, and discussion, but they can learn to *have* it and to *show* it only through your example and through your lavish praise of *their* example (or even of their attempts).

## GENERAL GUIDELINES

*Praise their attempts.* Reward the smallest evidence of courage in children of any age. By definition courage is hard. It usually requires the overcoming of a thumping heart and a mind full of uncertainty. When a child takes this step and makes a try, he deserves bounteous praise. And the praise should be for the courage to *attempt,* whether there was any success or not. Praise the trying of a new food, the speaking to a new friend, the attempt to build a difficult model, the reading of a hard book, the trying of an unfamiliar activity. Especially praise *moral* courage—not going along with others who were doing something wrong, telling the truth when a lie would have been easier, and so forth.

*Teach by your own example—show courage and point it out.* Give your children a parental model for courage. Tell your children about difficult things you do—not in a bragging or boastful way but in a candid way that lets them know that things are difficult for big people too. If you had a hard assignment, tell them about it. If you spoke to someone who had made you feel uncomfortable, tell them about it. If you said no to some peer pressure, tell them. Think of past things as well as current situations.

*Clarify the difference between courage and "loudness," and between the lack of courage and shyness.* This will help your children see that courage is a quality of character, not personality. If you have one or more particularly shy children, see that they understand that you are not trying to teach them to be louder or more assertive. Talk with them about *quiet courage*—the courage to say no to something that is wrong, the courage to say hello to a child who has no friends. Explain that everyone's heart pounds a little, that we're all a little scared, but that we *can* do what is right anyway.

*Help your children understand the makeup of courage.* The key to teaching courage to children of all ages is to realize that *preparation* and *faith* or *belief* (not just "red blood") make up courage. Our children will have courage if they are properly prepared, whether it is by thinking through decisions in advance and teaching them how to say no with confidence or by encouraging them to practice a piano piece for a recital and helping them to feel confident that they can perform well. Having faith in themselves to be able to do what they know is right is the key to courage. Children can realize that faith lies not in believing that something will turn up but in believing that *they* can *turn* something up.

## Methods for Preschoolers

### Praise the Attempts

Help your children to feel the joy of trying and to learn that courage is in the *attempts,* not in the accomplishment. If a little child is trying to learn to ride a two-wheeler, tie his shoe, or skip and can't quite get it, praise every attempt and assure him that he is getting better. Don't worry about the failures. Encourage the child to try again. Do all you can to help him succeed.

––––––

The first day our four-year-old got on his new two-wheel bike, he was thrilled beyond measure. He was so proud to go ten feet alone at first, then twenty. Finally he was riding all the way up and down our street. As the sun was setting on that

October afternoon and Eli was tired from a long day on the bike, he turned too quickly and fell on the pavement, smack on his two front teeth. They popped out like building blocks dropped on a hard kitchen floor, clean as a whistle. After an emergency trip to the dentist he was told that nothing could be done but that his toothless grin would only last a couple of years until the permanent teeth came in. The next morning, amid wild cheers from brothers and sisters, he was "back in the saddle again."

One sister told Eli how perfect he looked for Halloween, and another promised to teach him how to sing "All I want for Christmas Is My Two Front Teeth" for the upcoming holiday season.   —**Linda**

Looking back to our own childhood, we'd probably all find that some of our most courageous moments came on the heels of a failure from which we received encouragement to try again.

Remember, you can't overpraise! Attempts that are praised become the superstructure of deep and lasting courage.

### The Story of the Fast Heart

Telling the following story can help small children overcome the fear that often blocks even small acts of courage, and help them realize that it is normal and okay to feel scared:

> Betsy's heart was thumping. She was at swimming class, and her teacher wanted her to jump off of the diving board and swim to the side. She knew she could do it—she could easily swim that far, but it looked so far down to the water from up here on the board. She hadn't thought it would look this high. She wanted to

turn around and walk back off the board, but she also wanted to jump in and swim. Her heart was pounding.

Betsy took a deep breath and jumped. She plopped into the water and swam to the side. How great she felt! She had done it. She smiled from ear to ear.

The next weekend Betsy's dad took her to a movie. She had such a good time and on the way home she wanted to slide right over by her daddy and put her hand on his shoulder and tell him how much she loved him. But her dad was a very dignified and proper man and she wasn't sure he would like her to say that. Maybe he'd think she was "mushy" or silly and maybe he wouldn't say anything. But she wanted to put her arm around her dad and say, "I love you." She felt like it would be the right thing to do. Her heart was pounding as she sat in the quiet car, looking at her dad and trying to decide what to do.

She remembered that her heart had pounded before she jumped off the diving board—and she remembered how great she felt after she jumped. She slid over by her dad, hugged his arm, and said, "Thanks for the movie, Daddy, it was great. I love you!" Her dad, because he was a quiet man, didn't say much, but he put his hand on her arm and said, "Thanks, honey" in a lovely, warm voice. Betsy looked up and thought she saw a tear on her father's cheek. Her heart was still now, and she felt even better than when she'd jumped into the pool.

## Teach Them to Look People in the Eye

This can help children learn a useful habit that takes courage and that gives you a good opportunity for praise. Establish a family tradition of looking people in the eye. Explain to small children that if you look right at people, they will like you and know that you like them. Practice looking in each other's eyes as you say, "Hello," "How are you?" "Thank you," or as you ask questions: "Where do you live?" "What school do you go to?" And so on. Have little contests to see who can look into the other person's eyes the longest while having a "made-up" conversation. And have "staring contests" (who can look into the other person's eyes the longest without blinking).

Explain that being brave means not having anything to hide—and when we look right at someone, it is like saying, "I trust you and you can trust me." Learning to do this helps us not to be afraid to ask people questions or start conversations.

## The Dragon Story

The following story can help older preschoolers and young elementary schoolers relate storybook bravery to their own chances for everyday bravery:

> The young prince had never seen a dragon before, but he had heard of dragons and knew of their great strength and of the hot fire they could breathe out from their fierce nostrils.
>
> He was all alone the morning when the dragon came. He had gone for an early ride on his favorite horse and had just galloped down

the path and into the woods. As he turned a corner, he found himself face-to-face with the dragon (who was as surprised as he was). He could have turned his horse and run, and maybe he would have escaped, but the dragon was heading for the town, and surely others would be hurt or killed.

The young prince, his heart beating fast with fright, charged straight at the dragon while it was still startled and drove his sword deep into the soft valve on the neck that is used to draw in air to make dragon fire. The dragon was killed, the kindgom was saved.

Expand and elaborate this story as you wish. Then ask, "Did the prince have courage?" (Yes.) "Do we need courage today in this world?" (Yes.) "Why? We don't have dragons!" (Because there are other things than dragons that require courage.)

Make a list of "today's dragons"—things that take courage:

- Admitting you're wrong if you are
- Doing what's right when everyone else isn't
- Saying hi to a new child or a child you don't know
- Saying no when kids try to get you to do something you know you shouldn't
- Getting up early on a cold morning to practice the piano before school

## Methods for Elementary School Age

### The Leader-for-the-Right Award

Awarding this to a family member allows you to recognize and praise the courage children have shown. Have a "traveling" L.F.R. (Leader for the Right) Award that you give to some family member each Sunday at the dinner table. Ask, "Who is in the running this week for the Leader-for-the-Right Award?" Have family members (including parents) think back through the week just passed, trying to recall a time when they had a chance to stand up for what they believe—a time when "the crowd" was doing something wrong or dangerous or harmful and you said no or tried to talk them out of it, or a time when you did something right on your own, even if no one else was. Note: The Icebreaker Award on p. 214 is also a good reward of courage and bravery.

---

We were sitting in the family room one evening reading a bedtime story to six-year-old Noah and three-year-old Eli. The story was about a princess who kissed a toad and turned him into a prince. Noah had heard the story before, and when he came to the part where the kiss was about to occur, he had a question: "What if *she* turns into a toad?"

Two of the older children were listening in, and the question led not only to a good laugh but to a good discussion. Do we influence others or are we influenced by them? Do we have the courage to do what we think is right, hoping others will do the same, or do we end up becoming like them by doing what they do? —Linda

---

### The Red, Orange, and Yellow Game

This game makes it fun for kids to think about courage and its alternatives in various situations. Start with three pieces of construction paper or cards that are red, yellow, and orange. Ask children what they would do in various situations and hold up the color that their answer represents (red = courageous, orange = average or neutral, yellow = no courage, a little cowardly). Alternatively present the situation and have children see if they can give all three levels of answers. Use the following list of situations and add more of your own:

- You're offered drugs by a fellow student. Yellow—you take them. Orange—you don't. Red—you report the distributor to school authorities.
- You're given a difficult chance to take an advanced class in a subject you're good at. Yellow—you decline. Orange—you say, "Maybe next year." Red—you go for it.
- You see your grandparents for the first time in a year. You want to hug them, but there are a lot of people around and you feel embarrassed. Yellow—you stand there and look down. Orange—you shake hands. Red—you give them a big bear hug.
- A new child from another country comes to school for the first time. He probably doesn't speak English and he looks scared. Yellow—you ignore him. Orange—you wait until you see other kids talking with him and then you try it too. Red—you are the first one to talk to him.
- There is a tryout for the school musical. You like to sing, but none of your friends are trying out

because they think musicals are silly. Yellow—you don't try out. Orange—you try out for a minor part by yourself. Red—you tell your friends you don't think it's silly and invite them to try out with you, for a major part.

- You have a sweater that you like but it's different from the kind "everyone is wearing." Yellow—you put it away and beg for one of the kind everyone else has, even though you don't like them very much. Orange—you don't wear the old one or ask for a new one. Red—you wear the one you like.

- Make up your own—perhaps based on a real experience.

### The Story of Butch O'Hare

Tell the following story to give your children a sense of large-scale courage and true heroics:

In World War II a young pilot named Butch O'Hare was trying to get back to his carrier after his fighter plane had been damaged. His squadron commander had sent him back, feeling that his riddled craft was of little further fighting use and that O'Hare should get it back to the carrier while it would still fly.

Reluctant to leave the mission, O'Hare nonetheless followed orders and headed back toward the carrier. On the way, by chance, he intercepted a squadron of Japanese Zeros (fighter planes) flying from another angle toward the American carrier, which, without its own planes, would have little defense against them.

Despite his crippled plane, O'Hare engaged them in a dogfight and ended up shooting down six of them. Finally, when he had run out of ammunition, he began trying to fly directly into the remaining Japanese planes, hoping to knock at least one more down, even though it would cost him his own life to do so. The Japanese flight leader, seeing that he was dealing with a "mad man," with someone who had no regard for his own life, decided to retreat and flew off in the other direction. O'Hare had attacked them with the intent of sacrificing himself in the hopes that he could bring down enough of them to save the thousands of men on his carrier.

As it turned out, O'Hare was miraculously able to coax his battered aircraft back and land it safely on the carrier. He became one of the war's most decorated heroes. A few years later the airport in his hometown of Chicago was named O'Hare Field in his honor. It was to become the busiest airport in the world.

### "What I'm Good At"

This list will give children the necessary confidence to be bold about being themselves—and thus encourage them to develop their own creativity and individuality. Children with higher self-esteem are better able to be courageous.

Sit down with children individually and help them make a list of what they are good at—of their talents, skills, gifts, and aptitudes. Try to make a *long* list, including general and obvious things like "fast runner" or "good singer" to less-thought-about things like "good at keeping the baby happy" or "good at noticing beautiful things."

Be careful to list only things where a real aptitude exists. Don't flatter. If he's not good at baseball, don't list it (although you might list "good at trying hard at baseball").

When the list is done, think about it together. Ask the child, "Is there anyone else with exactly these same abilities?" Explain that he is unique, and no on else is quite the same. Build him up, make him feel special, and tell him *always* to be himself because his self is so unique and special. Encourage him never to try to be anyone else, because you like him and love him for what he *is*.

### *Hard* and *Good:* The Relationship Between Them

This activity will help children begin to relish rather than resist hard challenges. For this game set up two sides with at least one child to a side. Say that you are going to mention certain actions and you want one side to write either "hard" or "easy" to define each action. The other side should write "good" or "bad" about each action. (Each side needs a paper numbered from one to ten and a pencil.)

**1.** Get up early and study for a test.

**2.** Say you're sorry to someone even though it's embarrassing.

**3.** Try smoking with your friends so they won't call you chicken.

**4.** Make friends with the new kid at school, even though everyone else is ignoring him.

**5.** Sleep in on Saturday instead of getting up to do your household job.

**6–10.** Add your own (try to draw from real experiences).

When the game is over, match up the two team lists. Show how "hard" almost always matches up with "good."

## Methods for Adolescents

### Learn (Memorize Together) Shakespeare's Line "Our Doubts Are Traitors and Make Us Lose the Good We Oft Might Win by Failing to Attempt"

This kind of memorization exercise gives children a constant reminder that good impulses and ideas should be *implemented* even if we feel shy or inadequate or self-conscious.

Discuss with adolescents how often our doubts and insecurities can stop us from trying out for something or from acting on a good idea we have. Think of some personal experiences to share. Ask them to recall some. Reinforce the idea that trying and failing is better than not trying. Memorize some other quotes together (and discuss them both as you learn them and as they come up in later situations):

> 'Tis better to have loved and lost than never to have loved at all.
>
> Shakespeare

> A realization of the universal lack of self-confidence tends to strengthen one's own.
>
> Anonymous

In the battle of life, it is not the critic who counts—not the man who points out where the strong man stumbled or where the doer of the deed could have done better.

The credit belongs to the man who is *in* the arena, who does actually strive to do the deeds. . . . who, in the end, if he succeeds, knows the triumph of high achievement and who, if he fails, at least will never find his place among those cold and timid souls who never knew either victory or defeat.

Theodore Roosevelt

There are many causes I would die for—but none that I would kill for.

Mahatma Gandhi

### Courage and Its Opposites: Help or Hurt

This activity helps adolescents see *why* courage is a virtue and to focus on the *reasons* for developing courage. As usual with this method, ask for antonyms or opposites for *courage (cowardice, doubts, fear, tendency to blame others,* etc.). Discuss whom courage helps and how. Then discuss whom its opposites could hurt—and how.

### Decisions in Advance

This can help adolescents make right—and courageous—decisions *before* they are in situations conducive to wrong choices. Explain to adolescents that many decisions are best made early—before we're confronted with pressure to decide. Help them to make a list (preferably in the back of a journal or diary) of "decisions in advance." For example, I will not smoke. I will not cheat. I will not be cruel or rude even if others around me are, and so forth.

With each "decision in advance" help the adolescent to imagine a future situation where it would be very difficult to keep the decision. Think it through together. Point out how much easier it is to do the right thing when the decision has been made in advance.

To illustrate the point, tell them the story of Abraham Lincoln, who was riding in a coach with an important and influential man who was insistent that Lincoln smoke with him. He said he would be *offended* if Lincoln did not.

Abraham Lincoln said he had made a decision twenty years before not to smoke. He had committed himself to that decision and had even made the commitment to his mother. Because he had made the decision in advance, courage to keep it came easy for Lincoln, and his friend did not push him further.

### Encourage Children to Try New Things

Help your children develop a more daring attitude that will broaden their perspective. Encourage them to try something other than hamburgers and fries. Remind young adolescents that there are wide varieties of good things in life and help them adopt an adventuresome attitude toward things that are inherently safe. But also be sure to point out the difference between being daring and being foolhardy.

---

I was traveling on a short holiday with three of our children. It was during the years we lived in England and we had crossed over to France and stopped at a seaside restaurant. Trying hard to set a courageous and adventuresome example,

I looked over the menu and ordered something called "fruits of the sea" because it was highlighted as the house specialty. The kids, unimpressed and unaffected by my daring leadership, went ahead and ordered fish and chips.

When dinner was served, the waitress set in front of me an enormous two-tiered turntable-style plate covered with every imaginable variety of totally *raw* fish. There was squid, octopus, eel, and snails to go with the less terrifying oysters, clams, mussels, and lobster.

Recognizing that practicality is often the better part of valor and reminding myself that it wasn't the "month" for the value of courage anyway, I sent the "fruits of the sea" back and ordered a gourmet hamburger.   **—Richard**

### Make a List of "Everyday Ways to Show Courage"

This can help your children mentally practice the exercise of courage by thinking about common situations that would require it.

Make the point that courage is not something that is only useful on a battlefield or in great and momentous situations. It is an everyday thing. Say, "Let's use our imaginations for a moment and think of some common situations that require courage, and let's give a *name* to the *type* of courage that each requires."

Examples:

- Everyone else is wearing a style you don't particularly like. You decide to wear what you like rather than following the crowd. (The courage to be yourself.)
- Everyone eats lunch in the hall of the school. It's a nice day and you want to eat outside. Your friends won't go out, so you go out alone. (The courage to do what *you* like, even if it's by yourself.)

- You're with three friends who want to shoplift a couple of small things "just for the excitement of it." You say no, and they ridicule you. (The courage to do what's right.)
- You notice a new student in English class. He's sitting by himself and looks lonely. You go over when class ends and ask him about himself and make friends. (The courage to be friendly and overcome embarrassment or shyness.)
- There is an essay contest at school. None of your friends is entering it, but you would kind of like to. You've never entered a writing contest before and you're not sure you're any good at it, but you decide to give it a try. (The courage to *try*.)

---

Shawni, our very conscientious but rather shy daughter, was determined one semester to continue her near-perfect junior-high grades and stay on the honor roll. There were two classes she was very unsure of, and as the term drew toward its close, she was worrying about them almost constantly. "Go and ask your teachers where you stand," I told her. "Tell them you are trying for a four-point grade average and need to know if there's anything extra you can do."

"But it's so embarrassing, Dad. It's hard to ask teachers things like that." I told her that when I was a teacher I *loved* it when students wanted to do well and asked me how they were doing. Finally Shawni mustered up the courage. The teachers were helpful and she was able to get her A's.

It has become something of a symbol of the rewards of doing what is hard, and it's now Shawni who is advising her younger siblings to ask their teachers frequently where they stand on their grade.   **—Richard**

---

### Catch Your Children Being Courageous—and Praise Them

This will nourish and fertilize their development of courage. We can't force courage on our children, and we can't give it to them. They must find it for themselves and within themselves. We can help this process by discussing courage, noticing courage, and praising it to the hilt whenever it occurs.

### See the Movie *Chariots of Fire*

Watching this movie offers an excellent opportunity to give children clear and memorable images of particularly valiant and difficult courage. Watch the movie or video together. Discuss its several illustrations of courage, particularly the one when Eric Liddell stands up for what he believes before the king of England. Look for other videos or movies that illustrate courage. Another favorite of ours is *A Man for All Seasons*.

# Month 3:

# **Peaceability**

*Calmness. Peacefulness. Serenity. The tendency to try to accommodate rather than argue. The understanding that differences are seldom resolved through conflict and that meanness in others is an indication of their problem or insecurity and thus of their need for your understanding. The ability to understand how others feel rather than simply reacting to them. Control of temper.*

———

One of the new channels that suddenly turned up on our TV shows old movies and old TV series episodes all day long. I walked in one Friday afternoon (weekend time—when TV is on-limits at our house) and found the kids engrossed in *Ozzie and Harriet.* As usual with that show (memories flooded back), not very much was happening. No car chases, no murder plots, not even any soap opera drama. I sat down to watch. Ricky had some kind of problem at school which he was calmly explaining. Ozzie was putting his arm around Ricky and calmly saying, "Now, don't worry, son, we'll work this out."

When the show was over, I asked my eight-year-old if he liked it. "Yessss!" he said, "I like that show a lot. When is it on again?" When I asked him why he liked it, he thought for a minute and said, "It just sort of made me feel good." —**Richard**

---

Children need calmness. It gives them a kind of security. Peace and the control of temper is a powerful and important value that is largely a product of love and of the atmosphere created in a home! *Understanding* is the key. We seldom lose our temper when we are trying to understand. Children who are taught to try to understand *why* things happen and *why* people act the way they do will become calmer and more in control.

We have used the term *peaceability* to mean understanding, calmness, patience, control, and accommodation—essentially the opposite of anger, losing one's temper, impatience, and irritation. Just as there are a lot of ways to be dishonest, there are a lot of ways to be unpeaceable. Peaceability does not mean the elimination or ignoring of emotions. Rather, it means to *control* them and to prevent their causing hurt to other people.

Calmness and peaceability are values because they help others as well as ourselves to feel better and to function better. In addition to being values, they are contagious qualities. As you develop them within yourself, they are "caught" by others around you, particularly by your children.

## GENERAL GUIDELINES

*Create a peaceful atmosphere in your home.* Try to enhance the *setting* in which you live and teach this value. Improve the calmness of your home by: (a) playing restful music—much classical music creates a feeling of refinement, order, and peace; (b) controlling the tone and decibel level of your own voice—yelling accomplishes little and instantly punctures a peaceable atmosphere; (c) touching others in your family—we talk more softly when we touch; put a hand on a shoulder or arm as you speak to someone.

---

In our large family the "antipeace" reaches its peak about dinnertime. Everyone is talking, louder and louder, trying to be heard. Everyone needs something. The only way to get everyone's attention is to yell louder than they are yelling.

One day I happened to read a magazine article about the universal mantra *OM* chanted by Eastern meditators to calm their minds. When the noise started that evening at dinner, for want of anything better to do, I sat at the head of the table, breathed deeply, lowered my eyes, cupped my hands, and started chanting, "Ommmmmm."

Partly out of amazement and curiosity, the children fell into a hushed silence. Then there were questions. "What are you doing, Dad?" "Dad, don't you feel well?" Linda said, "Hold hands and do it with him." Willing to try anything once, they did, and for a couple of interesting minutes this usually boisterous and competitive family harmonized in a calm chorus of *ommmmmm*s.

We use that method almost every day now at dinner—to calm us all down, to get everyone to stop talking for a moment, to prepare us for the prayer of thanks we say before eating. It has become a collective way of saying "I love you" to each other and of setting the stage for a reasonably civilized evening meal together. An alternative is to simply have one minute of total silence before starting dinner. **—Richard**

---

*Set an example of and have an advance commitment to calmness.* Demonstrate the practice and the benefits of peaceability to your children and take advantage of the quality's "contagiousness." It is natural, as a parent, to say, "I have a right to get upset," or "They needed that." But no matter how much "right" we have, getting upset with children simply doesn't work very well, and children really don't "need" to see us lose our temper.

There is occasionally a place for "righteous indignation"—when children willfully and flagrantly do something they know is wrong. But too often our anger comes from our own frustration and sets negative and even dangerous precedents. Unfortunately anger, volatility, and impatience are as contagious as calmness. Children frequently exposed to it inevitably become frequent expressors of it.

———

Walking through a big shopping mall, we watched a little human drama that had a certain ironic humor but also a hint of real tragedy: A mother, walking along with her three children, got very upset when the little boy hurt one of his sisters. Slapping him sharply across the side of his head, she yelled, "I'll teach you to hit your sister!"  **—Linda**

———

Learn to preprogram yourself for calmness. Spend a quiet minute or two alone in your room (or in the bathroom) each morning before coming out to face the family. Decide in advance to react calmly to upset, feisty, or aggravating children. Do the same kind of self-programming when returning home from work.

---

I have a friend with a rather interesting method for avoiding any carryover of his work frustrations to his family and for helping himself respond peacefully to his family's needs. He pulls into the garage after a hard day at the office, pushes his automatic garage door closer, and then sits there in the dark car, imagining the worst scenario for what might be happening inside his home. He imagines that the house will be a mess, children will be fighting, his wife will look unhappy, and will have had a bad day at work, and no one will have started dinner. Then he imagines himself reacting calmly, helpfully, understandingly.

Then, he says, "I go in, and one of two things happens: Either it is exactly like I imagined and I react the way I planned or things are better than I imagined, in which case I feel happy and grateful."   —**Richard**

---

*Teach by praise.* Try to develop a "contagious calm" in yourself and to build it in children through positive praise.

Besides working to stay calm within ourselves, and trying to respond in a peaceful way, parents need to learn that "praise is peaceful" while "negative is nervous."

---

One summer I had the rare opportunity of spending three days in Scotland with our three oldest children. I had envisioned seventy-two blissful hours having these children all to myself learning wonderful things about history and culture, but it was not to be. One child didn't like Scottish food and couldn't think of any food but McDonald's (she claimed it sounded Scottish anyway); another child wanted to get up early and see everything; and another wanted to sleep. While one child carefully went through every room and read every sign in every castle, another wanted to hurry through everywhere in order to be able to see everything. I was disgusted with the picky eater, irritated with the squabbles, and disappointed that we had come such a long way to have a miserable time. I didn't mind letting the children know exactly how I felt. Angrily I pointed out everything that everyone was doing wrong.

That night I lay awake searching my mind for ways to change my children so that we could turn the fiasco into a festival. Suddenly I was struck with the thought that before I could change the children, I must change myself. Peaceability had to start with me. The next morning I began looking for things to praise instead of criticize about the children's behavior. I latched onto each little thing that was praiseworthy. "How did you get dressed so fast?" "Thanks for not complaining about sleeping on the cot. Tomorrow night you get the best bed!" "Your hair looks nice today," and so on. Like magic the mood became mellow. The more I expressed positive feelings and praise, the more children responded with smiles and sympathy for each other. I tried to respond to every negative remark with a positive one. By afternoon we had had one of the greatest days any of us could remember and certainly one that none of us will forget.

Once again I realized that I can often control the "peace barometer" at our house if I can just learn to control myself.  **—Linda**

## Methods for Preschoolers

### The "Calm Couch" and the "Repenting Bench"

These methods combine a penalty for temper and hurtful conduct with a way to get attention for improving. Have a hard bench or two straight-backed chairs somewhere in the home where children who fight are assigned to sit. Children who fight (physically or verbally) are sent instantly to the bench. A child can get off only when he can tell you what *he* (not the other child) did wrong and when he "repents" to the other child with a hug and a request for forgiveness.

Also have a particular couch or softer chair designated as the "calm couch" or "calm chair." When a child is fussy or feisty or loses his temper, have him sit in the calm chair until he is calm.

Don't treat the calm chair or the fighting bench as punishments—rather as ways to *avoid* punishment. If children *don't* wish to sit on the fighting bench to think about what they did wrong and apologize, *then* they get punished. If they don't want to use the calm chair to calm down, *then* they get sent to their room.

### Stillness Contests

This is a way to teach small children the *feeling,* as well as the skill, of being peaceful, quiet, and calm. Have contests to see who can go the longest without speaking, or without moving. Afterward say, "It feels nice to be quiet and still sometimes, doesn't it?"

### The Magazine Game

This game helps small children realize that it *is* all right to feel mad or sad, just as it is all right to feel happy or glad, but that it is *not* all right to hurt other people or their feelings because of how we feel. Flip through magazines with a child, stopping every time a person is pictured and asking, "How do you think he feels?" (Happy, jealous, worried, etc.—this is also a chance to teach children new words and the names of new emotions.) Then say, "Is it okay to feel this way?" (Yes.) Then say, "Is it okay to be mean to someone else if you feel mad or sad?" (*No!*)

### Explain "Temper"

Give your children the vocabulary they need to talk about anger and give them a way to *conceptualize* why anger is dangerous and harmful. Show children a pan of cool water. Have them touch it and put their fingers in it. Then put it on the stove over heat. Explain that when we get mad and lose our tempers, we start getting hot. When the water is boiling, say, "This is like getting angry and losing our temper—we get all bubbly and upset and we can hurt people. Would you like to touch that water now?" (No!) "So let's try not to boil—not to get mad, not to lose our temper."

### Counting to Ten

This helps young children learn a practical *method* for controlling their tempers. Since preschoolers are excited about learning numbers and learning to count to ten, explain to them that there is *another* reason (besides adding, subtracting, etc.) for knowing numbers and how to count. It can also help us control our tempers. Explain how counting to ten before we yell or get angry allows us to calm down. Go through some examples—situations where something makes them mad—talk about what would happen if they got mad, and what would happen differently if they counted to ten first.

Set the example by letting your children see (and hear) *you* counting to ten.

### A Simple Musical-Harmony Game

This game can help older preschoolers get the idea of harmony. If you have a piano, show children the difference between a chord that is in tune and in harmony and the sound of two or three random and dissonant keys struck together. Let them hear the sound and say,

"Harmony" or "No harmony." Then ask which sounds best. Then ask which sounds the most like peace and calmness and which sounds upsetting. Finally talk about the other (but similar) kind harmony—of how people treat each other.

## Methods for Elementary School Age

### The Peace Award

This award is a good way to praise and recognize children for their efforts to stay calm and peaceable. Make up a Peace Award by lettering the word *peace* or the symbol on a card. Remember that awards get posted on the bedroom door of the family member who wins it for the week. Using the Sunday-award technique discussed in earlier chapters, say to children, "Who is in the running for the Peace Award?" A child might be in the running if he has not lost his temper, has not retaliated when someone hurt him, has counted to ten, or could explain *why* someone might have done a hurtful thing.

Lavishly praise every effort. Be in the running yourself, thinking of examples of your own efforts to be peaceable during the week just passed. Discuss each situation that anyone brings up.

Give the award to the family member who has made the greatest effort to be peaceable that week. Praise the winner profusely!

### The "Two to Tangle" Concept

Help children see that the opposite of peace is fighting and that since one person can't fight by himself, both sides of a fight must be partly to blame.

Use the "repenting bench" (see page 81) with elementary-age children as well as with preschoolers. Explain to children that if they are peaceful and refuse to *retaliate* (learn the definition of this word together), then there can't be a fight.

### "Technical Fouls"

This method can help sports-oriented kids see the benefits (and adopt the goal) of calm behavior. Sports-minded kids who know about technical fouls and the sign the refereee gives to call one (straight, vertical, right hand hitting straight, horizontal, left hand to make a *T*) are quick to understand why a "player" shouldn't lose his temper. In basketball you don't slam the ball to the court, push someone, yell at someone, or show disrespect or temper. If you do, you are hit with a *T*.

Set up a system in which every time you slap a child with a "technical," it costs him something (a small part of his allowance, a mark against his getting the Peace Award, etc.).

### The Color Game

This is a good way to teach younger elementary-aged children the good consequences of peace and the bad consequences of anger and retaliation. Cut out two single figures in the human shape, one from red paper and one from some pastel color. Tell the children that the red represents temper and impatience, the pastel is control and peace. Give them a situation and let them tell you what each figure might do in each of the following situations:

- Your alarm clock doesn't go off, so you're going to be late for school.
- You're playing basketball and you get called for a foul you didn't think you committed.
- Your friend forgets to meet you for lunch.
- Your little brother flips you with a rubber band.
- Your mom says you can't have a sleepover because there's school tomorrow.
- The new pen you just bought won't work.
- And so on. Think of your own, based on your own experiences.

———

One year we were so busy in January that the Christmas tree just didn't get taken down. On a Saturday, early in February, I finally got around to the task. As I was "undecorating," eight-year-old Saydi walked in. "Oh, don't take it down, Dad!"

"Saydi, it's February, it's got to come down."

"But there's such a nice feeling here when the tree is up, Dad. It's all peaceful and warm feeling. I wish our house would feel like this all year long."

A week or so later I bought a small artificial Christmas tree (it was on sale, since it was February). Every once in a while, when things seem hectic and strained, I set up the little tree for a day or two.   —**Richard**

———

### Memorizing

Teach your child a phrase that will help him *understand* rather than *argue*. Have children memorize the couplet "A man convinced against his will is of the same opinion still." Help them understand the simple meaning that even when we win an argument, the other person resents us, so it is better to try to understand the other person and find a way to agree. Another good saying to memorize comes from Keats: "Beauty is truth, truth beauty,—that is all ye know on earth, and all ye need to know." Discuss how beauty is more visible to those who are calm, peaceful, and truthful.

## Methods for Adolescents

### The "Analytical-or-Angry" Discussion

Help young teenagers conceptualize the benefits of trying to "understand" rather than trying to "win." At dinner or some other natural conversation time make the statement that we have many situations in which there is a choice between two *A* words—arguing or analyzing. In other words, when someone does something to us or says something with which we disagree, we can either fight back and argue *or* we can try to *analyze why* he did or said it.

Point out the second choice is better because we *learn* something whenever we try to figure out why, and we keep our cool and keep our friends.

### Story and Follow-up Discussion on the Theory of "Win-Win" Situations

This exercise will help adolescents begin to see the world not as constant competition and "win-lose" but as a place where understanding can help everyone win. Tell this brief incident: Holly and Mary had been friends for years, but they were both strong-willed, so they had frequent disagreements. In their history class one day the teacher asked students to pair up and then choose one of the topics listed on the board for a dual report given by the paired students that would count for half of their grade. Holly and Mary teamed up but couldn't agree on a topic. Holly wanted one and Mary wanted another. They began to argue about it, and then Holly, remembering something her mother had told her, decided just to *listen* to Mary. It turned out that Mary had a very good reason for wanting a particular topic—and that she had some special information that would help make a good report on it. As Holly listened, she thought of some ideas she could add. The girls agreed on a topic and ended up getting an A on their report.

Ask what the difference is between "win-lose" and "win-win." Define "win-win" (finding a way to agree—a way where no one is hurt and where everyone benefits). Think of other examples.

### Share Your Method of Prethought

Flatter adolescents by suggesting that you and they adopt the *same* method for becoming peaceable. Discuss the "preprogram" idea (from the general methods section of this chapter). Help kids develop their own way of deciding in advance to be calm.

### Explain with Candor the Natural Moodiness Caused by Puberty, Hormones, and So On

It's important to help adolescents better understand and accept their moods. Young people's ability to be peaceable is often affected not only by their physiology but by their *concern* over it. A candid discussion about how the hormones of adolescence can affect moods can help children better accept their own change and emotions. Explain that it is natural in adolescence to feel great one moment and lousy the next. Explain that it's all right—and that the only thing to worry about and work on is being sure that our moods don't hurt others unduly.

*Month 4:*

# Self-Reliance
# and Potential

*Individuality. Awareness and development of gifts and unique-*
*ness. Taking responsibility for own actions. Overcoming the*
*tendency to blame others for difficulties. Commitment to per-*
*sonal excellence.*

———

Our fifteen-year old daughter, true to her age, her hormones, and her nature, had spent the evening alternating between hot anger, cool sullenness, agitated irritation at other family members, and woeful, sorrowful withdrawal. "I'm going to flunk math because the teacher is so weird. He never explains anything. He grades way too hard. He never calls on me when my hand is up. I don't care anyway, grades are way too important to most people. Actually it's my brothers and sisters who are ruining my grade. They're so loud and noisy, I can't study around here. Forget about an A. A B- is okay. It's not best, but it's good, and no one should be dissatisfied with good. If you'd been around more to help me study, maybe I wouldn't be in this mess." It was a not-so-rare collection of statements illustrating self-criticism and the blaming of others that goes on so often with some adolescents. But it wasn't our daughter's truest self. We had learned that at such moments there was little to do but wait for that truer inner self to emerge.

It finally did, about ten-thirty. "I'm sorry, Mom and Dad. That was stupid. It's my class and my grade. It's my own fault about the last test. I'll go see if I can make it up. I know I have the ability to get an A."   **—Linda**

Jekyll and Hyde? So many adolescents are. The challenge for parents is to encourage the Jekyll and help it win over the long run.

There are two separate but closely related principles involved here. The first is the *self-reliance* of accepting the responsibility for and the consequences of one's own actions and performance, rather than blaming luck or circumstances or someone else. The second is trying to be one's best self and asking the best from oneself—the conscious pursuit of individuality and *potential*—and the conscious rejection of avoidable mediocrity.

"Self-reliance and potential," as we have called it, is a powerful value. Those who have it help others by accepting responsibility and doing their best in the world. Those who don't have it hurt others by blaming them and by failing to develop the gifts and talents that could serve or enlighten or benefit other people. One who reaches his potential *helps* others in many ways as he develops himself. One who never seeks his full potential indirectly *hurts* others by *not* doing the good or setting the example he is capable of.

This value is about trying to know ourselves, to do

our best, and to accept the consequences both of who we are and of what we do.

One way to think of self-reliance and potential is as two sides of the same coin. Self-reliance has a lot to do with *taking the blame* or the responsibility for negative things that happen. Potential has a lot to do with *taking a little credit* and taking the right kind of pride in what we are able to become and what we are able to accomplish.

When we take blame and responsibility, we resolve and grow and improve. When we don't we become bitter, jealous, and defensive. When we take positive pride in what we're doing with ourselves and our gifts, we feel the growth of individuality and self-esteem. When we don't, we tend to become followers or plodders in the standard ruts of life.

## GENERAL GUIDELINES

*Use yourself as the model and example.* Show your children that you "value this value" and that you work for it. Take every opportunity to show your children how *you* are trying to improve. Talk about the things you think you're good at and working to be better at.

Show pleasure in things you do well. Also, be obvious about taking the blame for mistakes you make. Say, "You know, that was my fault. Here's what I could have done differently. . . ."

Let your children see that you can accept responsibility and blame and let them see that you take pride in who you are and that you are working to be better.

*Watch your children.* Try to recognize their gifts and help them develop their unique individuality. We must *know* potential before we can reach it. Children are not interchangeable "lumps of clay" that can be molded into whatever we please. Rather, they are "seedlings" that have their own separate and distinct gifts and potentials. We can never change an oak into a pear tree. But we can watch and recognize as early as possible who they are—and then nourish and encourage them to be the best of whatever they are. As parents we must consciously commit ourselves to finding out who our children truly and deeply are rather than trying to conform them to who and what we wish they were or to extensions of our own egos.

It is tragic that, despite our professing that our children are our highest priority, the average parent spends only seven minutes per day with an individual child.

*Praise.* Reinforce your children's self-image and individuality and build their confidence—that is required for self-reliance. Like flowers under rain and sunshine, children blossom and bloom under recognition and praise. "Catch them doing something good" and when you do, give effusive praise! When they make mistakes or fall short, help them accept responsibility for it and then praise that acceptance to the point that their pride in their self-reliance outshines their concern over the shortcoming.

## Methods for Preschoolers

### The "Repenting Bench" Revisited

This method helps small children take responsibility for their own actions rather than blaming others. The "repenting bench" (from month 3, "Peaceability") is a technique to correct any form of fighting (from physical to verbal). It involves sitting the two "opponents" on an uncomfortable bench and allowing a child to get off only when he can tell you what he (not the other child) did wrong. In addition to being a way to end fights, this is also an exercise in self-reliance and in accepting responsibility rather than blaming others.

### Natural-Consequence Punishments and Rewards

These can help preschoolers understand that their actions produce good and bad consequences. Try to set up a system in your family that fosters self-reliance by relating rewards and punishments directly to performance. The example that follows may not fit for you, but it may help you adopt a system that works in your family.

———

For years now the meaning of responsibility in our family has revolved around the pegboard that each child has in our kitchen. There are four big blocky pegs hanging from small chains for each child. He can put his first peg in when he has done his "morning things" (made his bed, brushed his teeth, come to breakfast on time, etc.). He can put in his second peg when he has done his daily household job (a very simple job for a preschooler, such as pushing the chairs in after a meal). He can put in his third peg when he has practiced. (They practice their musical instrument when they are old enough to take lessons. Before that age they practice reading basic words or drawing or some other simple skill.) He can put in his fourth peg when he has done his "evening things" (brushed his teeth, gotten ready for bed on time, etc.).

At the end of the week have a Saturday "payday." The amount of the child's allowance is determined by how many pegs he put in. (Children keep track by putting a number on a slip of paper each day—the number of pegs put in—and getting Mom or Dad to initial the slip.)

This peg system is primarily for elementary-age children. We don't push preschoolers into it. But when a four- or five-year-old begins to *want* an allowance, to *want* a family job, or to *want* to study music, we give him a pegboard and get him started.

On "payday" at the end of the week there is no criticism of a child who has not put many pegs in. Rather there is *praise* (along with the monetary reward) for any child who *has* been self-reliant and taken the initiative necessary to get the reward.   **—Richard**

———

Set up your own family system for responsibility. Keep in mind that the simpler your system is, the better it will work. Be conscious of helping children to see that it is *their* actions that determine both the "good" and the "bad" that happens to them.

### Give Your Children Opportunities to Do and Decide Things for Themselves

This will help small children gain the beginning sprouts of self-reliance and self-confidence. As much and as early as possible, let children dress themselves, do small household jobs, decide which shirt to wear or which color of juice to drink, get themselves in and out of cars, highchairs, and so on, and help you even when it would be easier without their help. As they accomplish even the smallest things, praise them and emphasize their ability to do things for themselves and by themselves.

### Keeping "Records"

This is a good way to help young children feel the joy of improving on their own. Competitive instincts generally begin to run high in four- and five-year-olds. If these drives are too focused on winning over or beating others, lots of insecurity as well as intolerance can result. Help children learn the concept of competing with *themselves* by setting up some simple "personal records" (anything from how fast they can get ready for bed to how far they can throw a ball). Let them try to beat their *own* record—not to compare themselves with others. In this type of activity you will find many opportunities to talk about doing one's best, practicing, trying, improving, and so on. With older preschoolers you can even introduce the term *potential* and help them understand that the word means *looking for our own best.*

### Praise Creativity and Emphasize Individuality and Originality

Help your children to like their own unique selves. Just as small children need to hear the sound of letters over and over and over again before they learn to read, so also they need to hear their own unique abilities praised time after time before they actually believe in themselves and increase how much they like who they are. Simple as it sounds, the key "connection" of this chapter is that children who like themselves become capable of relying on themselves, of accepting responsibility, and of reaching for their full potential. Praise every effort you see them making—from drawing a picture to trying to tie their shoe. Look constantly for new things they learn to do or for any sort of aptitude at which they seem particularly good.

Help a child see that he is unique by making up an "I am special" book with a front cover tracing his silhouette, and with his height, weight, eye color, favorite food, funnest activity, best skills, and so on written inside. Help him understand that there is no one, anywhere, who is exactly like him.

Help children to learn to say, when they face something they can't do, "I can't do————, but I can do————." This will help them later on to accept their weak points *with* their strengths.

### "The Good-Sport Game"

This game helps teach small children the principles of sportsmanship and of not blaming others. To set up this simple game, you will need a pair of dice—actually one die will do; a kitchen pan with either a bean bag or some other soft object to throw into it, and any gameboard with markers that move around it from start to finish. (A Monopoly board will work, or you can make up a simple board on cardboard or paper that has about fifty spaces from start to finish.)

Each child on his first turn tosses the die and moves his marker the number of spaces (from one to six) that comes up. On his second turn a child tries to toss the beanbag into the pan from a few feet away. If it goes in, he moves his marker six spaces. If it hits the pan, but doesn't go in, he moves four. And if it comes close, he moves two. On his third turn he rolls the die again; on his fourth he tosses the beanbag again, and so forth.

It is your *discussion* during the after this game that teaches principles of sportsmanship and self-reliance. When a child rolls the die, say something like, "What did you get?" (A three.) "Is that good?" (I guess.) "Is it as good as a six?" (No.) "Whose fault is it that you didn't get a six?" (Nobody's.) "It just happened, didn't it? Some things aren't anyone's fault. Should we be upset when we get a three, or a one?" (No.) "That's right. You'll probably do better next time. Let's just be happy we're all playing the game."

When a child throws the beanbag, ask questions like, "What did you get?" (A one, because I came close.) "Do you wish you'd get a six?" (Yes.) "Whose fault is it that you didn't get a six? Is it the beanbag's fault?" (No.) "Is it the pan's fault?" (No.) "Is it Billy's fault for laughing when you tossed." (No, not really.) "Is it your fault?" (I guess.) "But you tried, didn't you?" (Yes.) "Then it's not anyone's fault, is it? You'll just try again next time."

As a child gets a high roll say, "Oh, good—lucky for you." And as he gets a low roll say, "Oh, well, better luck next time." As he does well with the beanbag, say, "Good job." And as he missed, say, "Nice try." Encourage other children to say the same kinds of things.

When one child wins, be sure you and the other players congratulate him, and make sure he is a good winner and says, "I was lucky. Maybe you'll win next time." Be sure good losers are praised as much as good winners. Tell them that in the Good-Sport Game everyone wins who is a good sport no matter where his marker is on the board.

Introduce the term *good sport*. Explain sportsmanship as being a good winner *and* a good loser who doesn't blame other people for what happens. Explain why everyone loves a good sport.

Then watch for chances to compliment children on any good sportsmanship they show in normal activities.

## Methods for Elementary School Age

### Give Initiative—and Don't Take It Back!

Let the laws of natural consequences work in your children's day-to-day lives. As children turn seven or eight years old, try fully to implement the peg system described in the preceding section. Be sure they understand that the amount of their allowance on "payday" will be determined by how many pegs they put in. Encourage and remind them about their pegs for the first couple of weeks, but then sit them down and explain that from now on "it's up to you." You'll not be thinking about it or reminding them. If they remember and if they take the initiative, they'll be rewarded and happy on payday. If they don't, they're likely to be sad and left out on payday.

Have the patience to let them suffer the "no money" consequences of forgetting, of procrastinating, or of inconsistency in getting their pegs in. Say, "Whose fault is it?" and help them to see that it all depends on them, that they can do better next time and that they can be self-reliant!

### The Self-Starter Award

Each week during this month, perhaps at the Sunday dinner table, present the Self-Starter Award to the family member who has taken the most initiative (acted without being asked or reminded) in getting his job done, pegs in, homework done, and so on. As always with awards, ask, "Who thinks they're in the running for the Self-Starter Award for last week?" Help them think through and review the week just past and praise them for every instance of self-starting or initiative-taking. Be sure they understand that self-starting means doing things without being asked or reminded and doing *more* than was expected or "going the extra mile."

### Let Your Children Buy Their Own Clothes

This can help children feel both the pleasures and the pitfalls of taking responsibility and being self-reliant. Once children have a way of earning their own money (the peg system just discussed), they should also have some responsibility for what they do with that money. Having them buy all their own clothes and personal effects with "their money" can provide tremendous learning experiences.

———

In our family, when a child turns eight, we take him on a special "mommy-daddy date" to a nice restaurant and essentially induct him into the world of self-reliant adults. We tell him how proud we are of him and flatter him by telling him that we think he is now old enough to earn more money from the pegs, to help more with the smaller children, *and* to start choosing and buying all of his own clothes with his own money.

They certainly make mistakes. Sometimes they spend more than they should on certain things. Often they spend too much and save too little. They buy things they'll have little chance of wearing and forget things they really need.

But they *learn*. Experience and trial and error are extremely swift teachers. The bottom line is self-reliance. And we've come to believe that the mistakes of eight-year-olds are not serious, while the mistakes of eighteen-year-olds who have just received responsibility can be deadly. In today's society, children are often given license too early and responsibility too late.

Eight is a marvelous and unique age. Eight-year-olds are old enough to take initiative and make thoughtful, reasoned choices, yet they are young enough to be flattered by responsibility and to accept it without the cynicism and resistance of children a couple of years older.   **—Linda**

### Consult Rather Than Manage

Put *yourself* in a role that maximizes your children's development of self-reliance and self-knowledge. Try not to take initiative away from your child. Suggest rather than command wherever possible. Ask if he needs help rather than forcing it on him. Try to notice what he likes and where his natural gifts and abilities lie rather than trying to decide what he will do and what he should be good at.

When he asks you to do his homework, say no. But tell him you'll check it after he's done and tell him if it's right and help him on the parts he's tried to do but still doesn't understand.

As children are old enough to understand the terms, tell them that you want to be their *consultant* and not their *manager*. Explain that they are the ones who have to decide what they will do and how well they will do it and that you want to help but not force. (Be sure they can separate this consulting help and guidance that relate to their *choices* from the laws and absolutes that govern their *behavior*.)

### Memorizing

Plant the concepts of self-reliance and full potential in your children's minds. There is a simple song from a little-known children's manual that we are very fond of. The first verse goes:

*I'm the one who writes my own story*
*I decide the person I'll be.*
*What goes in the plot, and what does not*
*is pretty much up to me.*

Have your elementary school-age children memorize these lines. Explain the meaning and the writing
metaphor. Discuss two basic questions in connection
with the saying:

- If something doesn't go just right for us, who is
  usually to blame? (Ourselves.)
- Why is it important to be the best we can be?
  (That's how we write the best story.)

A second phrase that could be memorized during
this month is *"Good—the enemy of best."*

Older elementary-age children will appreciate the
interesting and somewhat subtle meaning of this phrase
and will enjoy a discussion about how being content
with "good" can keep us from discovering our very
best. You might use some examples that compare good
with best—a school grade of B instead of A, just "getting by" on our music lessons instead of learning the
pieces perfectly, and so forth.

(Note: One way to motivate memorizing is to offer
"extra points" on the peg system described earlier in
this chapter. For example, a child who learned the saying
might be able to add one or two extra pegs to his total
during the Saturday payday.)

### Emphasize Sportsmanship

Help your children consciously define sportsmanship as doing one's best and being gracious and blaming

no one but themselves for the results. As elementary-age children become involved in sports and other competitive activities, take every opportunity to praise *effort* and *sportsmanship*. Emphasize these two things far more than winning. Help children see that it is immature to blame others and mature to accept an outcome and be gracious to one's opponent. Once again praise self-improvement and *trying* and deemphasize winning and losing.

## Methods for Adolescents

### The Gift List

This method is similar to "What I'm Good At" from Month 2, but with a twist. It will help young adolescents appreciate their uniqueness and will give you an opportunity to give them specific praise. Pick a segment of time when you are alone with your child—perhaps while driving somewhere together—and discuss his specific gifts and talents. Ask him what he thinks he's particularly good at. Tell him your observations about his attributes and aptitudes. Be as specific as you can. Little things ("you always keep your school books in order") are as important as big things ("you have a great aptitude for math—for anything quantitative").

Let the discussion evolve into how unique each person is and how important it is, especially as we get older, to value and appreciate what we are rather than to waste time envying others.

### The Problem List

This method can help adolescents focus on their shortcomings without inducing insecurity. *Following* your discussion of gifts, ask your adolescent what he considers to be his greatest weaknesses or problems. Keep your tone academic as well as interested. Do not imply either criticism or pity. *Listen.* Don't say too much.

Help him realize that each problem or concern he thinks of *does* have a solution. There are things we can *do* about each of them. We can rely on ourselves (and on our faith in a higher power) to literally change who we are.

### Discussion of Politics

This works to help adolescents see the practicality as well as the honor in accepting blame rather than making up excuses or cover-ups. At dinner or some other opportune time see how much your children know about Watergate and about the Iran-contra affair. Help them with details if necessary so that they know that Watergate involved a break-in and some illegal acts followed by a cover-up, and that Iran-contra involved selling arms illegally to Iran and funneling proceeds to the contras in Central America.

Ask if both the break-in and the arms sales and fund diversions were illegal. (Yes.) Ask what the difference was in how the two presidents responded (Nixon made excuses, participated in a cover-up, was not able to accept blame and be self-reliant in terms of admitting his mistakes. Reagan accepted blame and apologized publicly—to some extent at least—for mishandling or being ill informed of events.) Did the public judge the two men differently? (Most certainly.) How could this principle apply to us? (Discuss.)

### Reassure "Late Bloomers"

This can help slow-maturing adolescents retain a good self-image. Have an open discussion with young adolescents about puberty and hormonal changes (as mentioned in the "peaceability" month). Include the point that each person matures on a different timetable. If you have a slow-maturing adolescent, assure him that he will catch up and that there are some advantages to a slower pace. If you can find the great Irwin Shaw short story "The Eighty-Yard Run," read it out loud together. It is the story of a boy who makes a great run in his first game and then finds everything else to be anticlimactic. It is a good story to illustrate the advantages of gradual development and progress.

---

One of our daughters is wonderfully persuasive and has school debate trophies as well as an undefeated record in family arguments to show for it! The only problem with this gift is that it lends itself so well to the making of excuses and makes it so very hard to admit fault, accept blame, or apologize.

One day we read a short article by C. S. Lewis on the difference between asking to be excused and asking to be forgiven. She was impressed with the difference and understood that the former involves little real effort and can push people farther apart. The latter creates a warmth that pulls people together.

We decided together that picking out what we have done that is wrong, and taking blame without excuse, is the essence of good human relations as well as the heart of self-reliance. **—Richard**

---

### Avoid Overprotectiveness

Build your adolescents' self-respect, self-confidence, and self-reliance. Have clear rules (curfew, etc.) but within these, trust your adolescents and make a point of telling them that you not only trust them but have confidence in their ability to handle themselves and the situations they find themselves in.

This principle applies to smaller children also. Too many well-meaning parents may prevent a skinned knee or even a broken arm by being overly protective physically, but in the process they may exert undue influence and diminish the feelings of self-reliance and self-control.

# Self-Discipline and Moderation

*Physical, mental, and financial self-discipline. Moderation in speaking, in eating, in exercising. The controlling and bridling of one's own appetites. Understanding the limits of body and mind. Avoiding the dangers of extreme, unbalanced viewpoints. The ability to balance self-discipline with spontaneity.*

———

"Mom, I'll get up, I promise, just *please* don't tell me again about milking the cows."

It was Saydi. She was ten, and I was waking her (for the third time that morning) to get up and practice her piano before school.

When I was her age, I really did have to get up to milk the cow—and the cow wouldn't wait. In today's urban setting, discipline is often a choice rather than a necessity. To get up, to get going, to be a self-starter and a self-motivator is neither easy nor common.

But Saydi did get up, she did practice, and she understands that self-discipline feels good and is its own reward.   —**Linda**

*Self-discipline* means many things: being able to motivate and manage yourself and your time, being able to control yourself and your temper, being able to control your appetites (and here the companion word *moderation* comes into play).

Self-discipline and moderation are two sides of the same coin. Self-discipline is pulling up and away from the laziness of doing too little. Moderation is pulling in and away from the excesses of trying to do or to have too much.

Discipline and moderation are profound and universal *values* because their presence *helps* us and others and their absence inevitably causes short- or long-term *hurt*.

These are values on which all parents must work personally. And it is our example, more than any other method or technique, that will teach this value to our children.

This year, as he approaches fourteen, our most undisciplined child is beginning to show great progress. Three years ago he simply could not remember to do his homework. On occasion when he did do his work, he couldn't seem to remember whether or not he'd handed it in. His thoughts were immersed in model airplanes, snakes and gerbils, and computer games. Nothing else mattered much to him. I was constantly nagging him to clean his room and "get his act together."

Then two fairly significant things happened to him: Our family moved to

England, and he was enrolled in an extremely disciplined school for boys, complete with a school uniform that included black wool pants, black leather shoes, gray socks, a white shirt, gray V-neck sweater, school tie, and blue blazer. Any boy lacking any part of his uniform was severely reprimanded. Not only that, each boy was required to take thirteen subjects, which included physics, chemistry, classical studies, and mythology. Not a bad schedule of classes for a seventh-grader! Each boy was required to carry an assignment notebook in the left-inside pocket of his jacket. Each class and the assignment for that day were to be carefully printed inside. Any teacher could stop any boy and ask to see his notebook at any time. If the notebook was not there or was not complete, the student was doomed to detention.

At about the same time, I decided that my relationship with this child was suffering because of my incessant reminders to practice, to clean his room, to get his homework done. I eased off, and decided that my communication and friendship with him were more important than the tidiness of his room.

This year this boy was transformed from a caterpillar to a lovely moth. (He can't really be classified as a butterfly, because his room still looks about the same—even though he cleans it up at least once a month now without being asked.)

I find little homework lists in the jumbled place he calls his room, and he just became an Eagle Scout and a member of the National Honor Society. Instead of thinking of him as a thorn in my side, I now regard him as one of my favorite people.   —**Linda**

---

## GENERAL GUIDELINES

*Teach by example.* Create a personal example regarding the value of discipline and moderation in all areas. Again, example is the number-one method. Make up your mind, especially during this "month," to control your temper, to save a percentage of your income, to live within your means, to eat moderately, and so on.

Make a point of all these things—talk about them (and *why* you do them) with your children.

*"Count to ten."* Help children—and yourself—stay in tighter control of your tempers. There is no more obvious and noticeable illustration of discipline than in the control of temper. Teach your children the simple principle of counting to ten before saying or doing anything when they feel anger. Give some "bad examples" of people who hurt someone because they struck out (or spoke out) without stopping to think. Give some good examples of people who were about to say something angry or to hurt someone in some way and then thought better of it while counting to ten.

Challenge children (and yourself) to count to ten *out loud* during this month whenever anger begins to rise in their feelings. You do it too. Let each other hear the "One, two, three," etc. and realize that *each* family member is struggling for better control.

*Maintain a family schedule.* This can give children the security of certain things that are predictable and the discipline of being sure that they are there when expected. Have a set breakfast time and a dinnertime. Have different times for different days if necessary, but put them up on some sort of poster and see if everyone can discipline themselves to *be there* during this month.

*Use the terms* discipline *and* moderation *frequently.* This will help children understand them and "connect" them to everyday behavior. When you pass up a second helping of potatoes, say, "I'm going to use *moderation* and not eat too much—it will help my waistline." When you notice a child getting his homework done, say, "There's *discipline* for you." Make the words the "theme" of your communications and your activities for the month.

*Set up "deals."* Add motivation to your child's efforts to discipline himself to accomplish goals. Having children set up certain objectives and attaching a reward to the accomplishment of those goals can give parents added opportunities for praise and can make children more conscious of consistently disciplining themselves to do things.

---

At our home in recent years the "deals" have been a great summertime motivator for self-discipline. Usually at the beginning of the summer we talk with the children about the things they'd like to accomplish by September. For some it may be to be a better tennis or basketball player. For others it may be to learn a certain piece on the piano or become more proficient on the violin. Still others know that reading is important but can't seem to make time for it. A "deal" gets its beginning when one of the children "proposes" some goals and suggests a reward. We usually modify the proposal and make a counteroffer. For example, our ten-year-old proposed the following deal last spring: "Make ten left-handed lay-ups every day but Sundays for two months; read one book every two weeks for two months; make bed five days each week for two months. Reward: $100 for school clothes." We countered with one book a week, bed made every day, and added two balanced meals (all four food groups) every day for two months. The ten-year-old accepted the counteroffer, made up a chart to keep track, and proceeded to "make his deal."

The deals vary according to the age of the child. Little children usually require "deals" on a short-range basis and need lots of reminders. Older children need to take responsibility without being constantly reminded. We've had some children who want the reward from "the deal" so desperately that they feel like Ulysses strapped to the mast of his ship. Even though they hear the siren songs (the distractions of their lives), they are ecstatic when they accomplish their goals knowing that the "ropes" that bound them are self-inflicted. **—Linda**

---

## Methods for Preschoolers

### Work Before Play

This is a good way to teach small children the beginnings of self-discipline. Assign a small, simple family job to three- or four-year-olds (e.g., turn off the upstairs lights, push the kitchen chairs in after breakfast, feed the dog). Insist that they do their job before they play or watch TV, and so on. Then praise them for doing the job, explain that it really helps you out, and begin to define *discipline* by telling them, "Discipline is when you are strong enough to make yourself do what you should."

### Set Bedtime and Wake-up Times

Help your small children get the feeling of being "on time" and of having their minds "stronger" than their bodies. Set definite bedtimes for preschoolers. Help them learn to tell time (or at least to know when the little hand is pointing at the seven, etc.) and challenge them to notice when it is bedtime and to discipline themselves to be in bed on time (you will still have to remind them, of course). Tell them that if they are big enough to get in bed on time, they deserve an alarm clock to get up on time with. See if they can wake up, turn off their alarm, and get to breakfast on time. Give lavish praise when they do.

### Pegs

This helps four- and five-year-olds begin to take the initiative in disciplining themselves. The pegboard method described in Month 4 has additional utility in teaching discipline. Review the procedure on pages 94 and 95 and use the month to reinforce "pegs and payday" as a permanent practice in your family. Explain to the children that *discipline* means getting things done without being asked.

### The "Too Much" Game

This game will get small children thinking about the concept of moderation and about its benefits. Explain that too much can sometimes be worse than too little. Say, "Let's play a game about too much. I'll say 'too much————,' and you say something that you wouldn't want to do too much of————, then say what 'bad thing' might happen from too much." For example,

Too much food. . . . You might get fat.
Too much exercise. . . . You might get too tired, or even injured.
Too much candy. . . . You'd get cavities, lose your appetite.
Too much television. . . . It keeps us from playing, studying, and other good things.
Too much catsup. . . . You can't taste the food.
Too much bathing. . . . You might wash your skin off.

As the last two illustrate, you can have some fun with the game. But the bottom line is helping small children begin to understand the value of moderation.

———

We were trying to explain the concept of discipline and moderation to our four-year-old, Eli, as it related to the watching of television, and having very limited success.

We have a fairly rigid "no TV" rule for weekdays, and this little guy was arguing that the rule was just for the schoolkids who had homework. "I don't start school till next year," he said, "so I should get to watch cartoons. All you ever let me see is 'Sesame Street.' "

Help sometimes comes from unexpected sources. Our very quantitative fourteen-year-old overheard the conversation and came in, spouting some statistics he had heard at school.

"The average American family has a TV turned on for nearly seven hours a day," he announced, "up from three and a half hours in 1970. At that rate a kid like Eli would see nearly forty thousand hours of TV by the time he was eighteen."

The complexity of that argument went way over Eli's head, but he idolizes his older brother so much that he gave up the argument!   **—Richard**

## Methods for Elementary School Age

### The Work-Before-Play or W.B.P. Award

Give recognition and emphasis to self-discipline. As with each of the other "awards," ask (at Sunday dinner), "Who's in the running for the W.B.P. Award?" Help children think of times during the past week when they did homework before friends came over or did their jobs before going out to play. Be in the running yourself by telling instances where you did what needed to be done before doing what you wanted to do. Discuss how much more you can enjoy playing if you've done the work first.

We have also tried an S.W.N.D. ("See What Needs to Be Done") Award to encourage children to look around and do things without being asked.

If you have temper problems in your family, design

another "control" or "ten" (for "count to ten") award, and discuss it and give it out in the same way on Sunday for the week just passed.

### Delay Gratification

Help your children understand the discipline, and pleasure, of waiting for and anticipating something. One of the tendencies that works so strongly against discipline is giving children too much and making it too easy for them to get what they want. Work out a "save up" program for children who want a new bike or a new toy. Help them discipline themselves to shop for the best price and to set a goal by which time they hope to have the item. Help them see how the discipline of planning and saving and waiting will bring results that impulsiveness and "splurging" would destroy.

### The Family Bank

A family bank (a large wooden box with a lock and a slot in the top for deposits works well) is a great teacher of frugality and discipline, especially if it pays high interest. Let children spend their own money, but explain to them the rewards and growth of disciplined saving. On Saturday "payday" encourage children to put a percentage of their pay into the family bank so that they can earn interest and save up for a major purchase such as their education. Calculate interest and add it to their account quarterly. Give older elementary children an old checkbook and check register so that they can withdraw or deposit money to the family bank (and can learn the financial process and procedures of money management). When they are twelve, let them open a real checking account at a bank with their own money, with you as a cosigner.

### The "Choose the *M* or the *A*" Game

This game teaches older elementary school children the fact that some things are okay in moderation but bad in excess—while other things are bad in *any* quantity or form. Make up, on three plain sheets of paper, a large *M* for "moderation," a large *A* for "avoid" or "abstain," and a large N.L. for "no limit" (describe and define the words). Then explain that you are going to go through a list of things and you want them to pick one of the three signs for each of the items you are going to mention. Then go through the following list, adding items of your own and stopping to discuss or ask questions about any on which the answer is not clear.

> Eating (*M*)
> Taking drugs (*A*)
> Reading (*NL*)
> Exercising (*M*)
> Watching television (*M*)
> Caring for others (*NL*)
> Name-calling (*A*)
> Smiling (*NL*)
> Drinking alcohol (*A* or *M*—your call)
> Drinking before driving (*A*)
> Playing at friends' houses (*M*)

### Memorizing

Plant the concepts of discipline and moderation deeper into your children's subconscious by having them memorize short phrases. We use two that are easy to memorize and important to remember. Both can be put on signs and thought about frequently during this "month."

One is "Do it" or "Do it now." The other is "Mind over mattress." Use one to overcome laziness or procrastination and the other to get up early for music practice, homework, or brief family meetings before people go their separate ways. (With older elementary-age children you might also discuss some modifications of the second phrase: "Mind over menu," "Mind over muscle," "Mind over matter.")

### Music Lessons

Education in music offers a clear challenge and focal point for self-discipline. This is not an easy way to teach this value, but it can be extremely effective. Although almost all parents would love to have their children involved in music lessons, the extent of discipline necessary to succeed is sometimes quite high. Most children are initially excited about learning to play an instrument. Those who are disciplined enough to get themselves on a routine practice schedule and stick to it are rare!

---

The parent walks a fine line here. I can clearly remember my mother standing over me while tears streamed down my face because I couldn't go out to play until my practicing was done. I remember her saying with firm conviction, "Someday you'll thank me for this!"

Although I spent many hours producing angry fumes and dumping gallons of tears, she was absolutely right! I went on to major in music in college and found that music added quality and depth and self-esteem to my life. **—Linda**

---

Starting children on a musical instrument often requires buying an alarm clock for the child to help him get himself up in the morning and lots of reminders of where practicing fits on the list of priorities of the home. Getting the practicing done often requires every reward, praise, threat, or bribe that parents can think of and then some.

---

I've learned that music is not worth destroying a relationship with a child over. One year I found myself nagging, pushing, pulling, and prodding one of our sons—who incidentally was quite talented in music—to the point where we really didn't like each other much. When I realized what was happening, I had him quit lessons, and immediately our relationship improved.

Now, after a year's break, he is back at the keyboard. After a long talk he agreed that he would try to discipline himself more to practice, and I agreed to discipline myself to quit nagging him about practicing. We're both doing better!

—Linda

---

Music-practice philosophy in different homes ranges from "You don't have to practice every day—only the days you want to eat" to "Practice while you can; enjoy it while it lasts." Decide where you belong on the spectrum and use it as a great way to teach discipline—for both parent and child!

### Teach Your Children How to Set and Reach Goals

This does not mean only on New Year's Day, although that can be a start. If you take the time to sit down with them and talk about their goals for the coming year, they can think of all kinds of wonderful things.

Sometimes they learn that their enthusiasm outdistances reality, but it is a good learning process.

On the first Sunday of every month encourage children to set goals for the month ahead. Weekly goals can also be set, even by children as young as three or four. (Drawing pictures of a goal is as good as writing them down . . . sometimes better.)

### Praise

Praise helps reinforce and perpetuate this value. This simple word is probably the most important concept in teaching values to children and is especially crucial for children who are trying to learn to discipline themselves. Instead of expressing irritation to children for not getting household jobs done, express honest praise and delight every time they *do*. Instead of saying to yourself, "I can't believe Jill is doing the dishes without being told," say something out loud, like "I can't tell you how much it lightens my load to have you see the dinner mess and get it cleaned up without even having to ask you to do it. You are getting so good at seeing what needs to be done and doing it on your own initiative!" The chances of the child repeating that act of self-discipline increases tenfold—on the spot!

The next time you walk through the family room and see two or three children playing nicely together, stop and tell them how it makes you feel, instead of getting angry at them when they argue.

Every attempt to give honest praise is a solid-gold investment.

## Methods for Adolescents

### The Extension of the *M, A,* and *NL* Game

With this game we generate discussion with adolescents about moderation and self-control. Expand the elementary-age method of choosing the *M* or the *A* (page 116) and include items like "staying out until curfew," "dating the same person," and any other issues in your current life with teenagers.

### Fasting

This can teach physical discipline and help your child gain experience in an elementary form of putting the mind in charge of the body. Pick a non-school day, perhaps a Sunday, and agree to fast as a family for twenty-four hours (dinner to dinner). Children will usually agree to this as a challenge and an experiment. Use the fast to discuss how two-thirds of the earth's population feels every day (hungry), but particularly use it as an occasion to discuss the good feeling that comes from disciplining appetites. Point out that with any appetite the body tells you to indulge but the mind can override the body and the emotions. Such an override is a good definition of discipline.

### Getting Up Early

This habit gives children an opportunity to feel the satisfaction of "mind over mattress" and gives parents another opportunity for praise and reinforcement. During this "month" try an early-morning "day-start" meeting where you meet for five minutes before breakfast to briefly review what each person in the family is doing that day. Set the time early enough so that you can hold a five-minute meeting and still have fifteen or twenty minutes for breakfast before the family member with the earliest schedule has to leave.

———

It's interesting how different (physiologically as well as mentally and emotionally) children in the same family can be. When we started having a brief "daystart" meeting in the mornings, a couple of our children were always there on time, while two others never showed up unless someone dragged them out of bed.

Some of us are larks, some are owls!

The two larks were always dressed and ready for school when the meetings started. For a while we pushed the owls to do likewise, but it just seemed to be too much for them.

Finally we decided to change the format to "come as you are." Kids that were disciplined enough to be up and ready had the advantage of being able to study or practice their music after the meeting before going to school. The two that usually came groggy and in their pajamas had to rush to get ready after breakfast.

We'll probably always have two owls and two larks, but at least we're learning about ourselves, and enjoying each other as we work on one type of discipline.

—Richard

———

## Learn to Make Decisions in Advance

This is a way to assist teenagers in making correct choices clearly and objectively rather than emotionally and erratically. A great many undisciplined and disastrous teenage decisions are made on the spur of the moment, yet their results can last a lifetime. Help adolescents actually think through in advance some of the decisions you can predict they will have to make over the next few years. For example, think through with them (verbally) a situation in which they might feel considerable peer pressure to try drugs, to get drunk, to become sexually involved. Be specific in actually describing scenarios and ask them to be specific in mentally rehearsing exactly what they would say and do in those situations.

If you didn't already do this in Month 2, suggest that your adolescent actually make a list (in a private place—perhaps in the back of his journal or diary) of the decision he has made in advance (e.g., not to do drugs or drink, not to become sexually involved, to finish high school and stay academically on course for college).

These advance decisions, thought through with your help and recorded with real intent in a teenage journal, can be remarkably effective safeguards and "route markers" for the right path of discipline and moderation.

### Agree on Policies for Discipline

Give your teenagers the limits that provide security, convince them of your concern, and give them opportunities for the exercise of discipline. Sit down with your adolescent and decide together on some guidelines and standards that will help him exercise discipline and moderation as he moves into and through his teenage years. Some suggestions:

- Decide on a curfew. There is really no need (or very seldom a need) for extremely late hours. An amazing percentage of problems occur after midnight.
- Limit the number of nights out. Limit television, limit things that need moderation. A mutually-

agreed-on limit will help a teenager to exercise discipline more easily.

- Date one person no more than twice in a row. Require a date with someone else before a third date occurs with the same person.

### Introduce a Simple Planning System

This can help adolescents manage their time and energy—and also promote the development of spontaneity as a companion to discipline. Try (for yourself) and teach your adolescent children the following basic daily planning system:

**1.** At the top of a planning page list one single priority for the day for work (or school), one for family, and one for self.

**2.** Then put a vertical line down the middle of the planning page, list the things you need to do that day (*including* the three priorities) by time (hour) on the left-hand side.

**3.** Leave the right-hand side of the page blank—then watch for spontaneous or serendipitous things (unplanned happy accidents) that are better or more worthwhile than some of what is on your list. Try to meet the three priorities and to do at least one or two spontaneous things each day.

Try this system together for a week or two. Then discuss your individual results in a family discussion.

# Fidelity and Chastity

*The value and security of fidelity within marriage and of restraint and limits before marriage. The commitments that go with marriage and that should go with sex. A grasp of the long-range (and widespread) consequences that can result from sexual amorality and infidelity.*

In the age of AIDS it is easier than it has been for many decades to agree as a society on the desirability of fidelity in marriage and the good sense of abstinence before marriage. Those who now agree practically are added to those who have always agreed philosophically.

Whether or not you agree *morally* with this value,

you do, as a parent, have the responsibility to deal in your own way with these critical issues.

Many parents who did not practice chastity or abstinence in their own youth are nonetheless hopeful and even anxious that their children will. This is not hypocrisy and shouldn't cause guilt. Today is its own time—with its own concerns and its own reminders. And the fact that some of us have learned from our mistakes ought to be the best reason why our kids do not have to do likewise.

It is hard to argue against the mental logic and the emotional benefits of fidelity within marriage. And positive commitments toward it can start to form in very small children.

————

When our children have their eighth birthday, they undergo something of a rite of passage, going from a kid to a semi-grown-up, from a tutee to a tutor, from someone who knew almost nothing about sex and reproduction to someone who could probably teach a course on the subject.

We begin several weeks before the child's eighth birthday, "priming" him by indicating that when he turns eight, he will be given some new privileges, some new responsibilities, and will learn about "the most beautiful and wonderful thing on earth."

When the big day arrives, we take the new eight-year-old on a private daddy-mommy date to a nice restaurant, making every effort to treat him with a new maturity and respect. As mentioned earlier, we give him some added responsibility in areas such as choosing his own clothes and earning more money by doing family chores. We express our pride in him and our appreciation of him.

Then we go home for the much-anticipated highlight of the evening: our private talk about the "most wonderful and beautiful thing on earth." In upbeat, positive terms we explain the facts of life using diagrams and pictures to explain reproduction. (We particularly like using the child's book *Where Did I Come From?*) We encourage questions; we ask him often if he understands; and we watch his expressions to be sure he's not only comprehending but appreciating what we are telling him.

Then we make a very strong point of how smart and how right it is to be careful how we use something as important and as miraculous as sex. We point out that something that special should be saved for one person—for the commitment of marriage, where it can be a wedding gift that has never been given before.

Children accept this idea very easily. It seems natural to them that something so private and so beautiful (and something so magic and powerful that it starts new babies) should be saved and used carefully rather than spent indiscriminately.

It is also natural to them to understand that after two people are married, sex is a bond and a special, private way of expressing love between them that should not be used outside of marriage.

We also talk about AIDS and of the dangers of misusing sex. And we use the standard "values formula" by discussing how and who is *helped* by being careful about sex and how and who is *hurt* when people are not careful about sex.  —**Richard**

---

Eight may seem like a young age for some of the discussion represented above, but it is the *right* age for two very important reasons: (a) to wait longer runs the risk (if not the likely possibility) that your child will learn of reproduction and sex in the negative and silly perspective of the other children who will tell them about things before you do; (b) eight years old is a natural and curious age when children can understand in a sweet, uncynical way.

One evening and one discussion, of course, is not enough. An evening such as we have suggested can establish the basics and open wide the door of trust that permits the subject to be one of ongoing openness and discussion.

Certainly the underlying philosophy involved in teaching children the value of fidelity and chastity is that sex is too beautiful and too good to be given or used or thought of loosely or without commitment. The opposite view of sex as a dirty or evil thing should be avoided and countered at every opportunity.

———

I sat in the library one day, researching some quotations for a manuscript I was working on. I was having a hard time keeping my mind on my work because I was thinking about one of my adolescent daughters and about my efforts to help her understand *why* chastity and sexual morality was something to be sought or valued. She was not rebelling against the notion or even disagreeing with it. But she was at the age where any restriction bothered her. She had asked, the night before, why there were so many limits on so many things.

And I had wanted to tell her that chastity, like any true value or virtue, is a positive thing that you *gain,* not something you give up.

I was looking through some G. K. Chesterton essays and I literally fell onto the words I was wishing for. They were in an essay called "A Piece of Chalk," in which Chesterton uses the metaphor of an artist who was sitting on an English hillside drawing on brown paper. He had all his chalks except white; he had forgotten to bring the white. Could he do without it? No, because white is not the absence of color. White spaces are not blank, they are put on by the artist and can be the most important element in his canvas. Should he return home for a piece of white chalk? Then he realized that he is sitting on chalk—England is *made* of chalk, he said. He broke off a piece from a white chalk rock and completed the drawing.

Virtue, in Chesterton's mind, was not a void or the absence of a wrong. It was the *presence* of a right. And he felt that values or virtues are the *light* and the key to putting beauty into the rest of life. In Chesterton's words:

> The chief assertion of religious morality is that white is a color. Virtue is not the absence of vices or the avoidance of moral danger; virtue is a vivid and separate thing. . . . Mercy does not mean not being cruel or sparing people revenge or punishment; it means a plain and positive thing like the sun, which one has either seen or not seen. Chastity does not mean abstention from sexual wrong, it means something flaming, like Joan of Arc.   **—Richard**

The two most important reasons that parents should be the ones to teach children about sex and sexual morality are: (a) parents can teach in a warm and loving way that avoids the sterile, factual, academic tone that predominates in school discussions and the silly or "dirty" connotation that often accompanies peer discussions; (b) when a parent teaches a child about sex, the intimate and personal nature of the subject creates a mutual sharing of trust and forms an emotional bond between parent and child.

## GENERAL GUIDELINES

*Make your own example of fidelity as obvious and noticeable as possible.* You can help your children see the importance that you place on this value as well as the happiness and security it gives you. Talk about commitment in personal terms. If you are a two-parent family, point out how the two of you belong to each other so that you don't need any other man or woman. Try to let children see the basic physical signs of love and commitment, such as holding hands or a kiss as you leave for work.

*Make sex and sexual maturity an open topic in your*

*family.* Maximize the number of opportunities you have to comment on the logic and benefits of chastity and fidelity and to permit concerns and problems to surface early rather than late. With children over eight (assuming that you have had your initial talk with them as suggested), do all you can to make sex an open and agreeable subject rather than something that is secret or off-limits or silly or embarrassing. It may seem difficult and unnatural at first, but these feelings are a sign that the subject needs opening up. Things you observe on television, movies, and music—or in articles or books—or in styles of dress—all present potential opportunities to make comments about what you think is appropriate or not appropriate, what things are moral in the sense that they *help* and what things are immoral (or amoral) in the sense that they may *hurt* someone physically, mentally, or emotionally.

Look for chances to discuss the behavior of young adolescents (your children's acquaintances) and bring up the possible connections of that behavior to hormones and the effects of puberty.

Strive to convey the following two impressions whenever possible: (a) sex, the feelings and changes of puberty, and the attractions and feelings they cause us to feel are *natural* and *good,* even *wonderful* and *miraculous;* and (b) because sex is natural and good, and because its urges are *powerful* and have to do with the creation of life, its use should be *connected* to love and commitment—it is too beautiful to be made common or to squander.

## Methods for Preschoolers

### Teach Them About Body Parts and Functions, Using the Correct Terms

Point out physical differences in boys and girls in order to begin to give small children an appreciation of their bodies and to introduce and implant the *openness* with which you want children to think and feel about their bodies. Use bathtimes to bring up the beauty of the body. Talk about the muscles and the bones, about how bodies grow and get stronger, about how sores and broken bones heal as good as new, about how boys' bodies differ from girls' and about how both male and female bodies are beautiful and miraculous.

### Answer Children's Questions to a Certain Point and Help Them Positively Anticipate Other Answers When They Turn Eight

Encourage questions and openness and emotionally prepare your child for the eight-year-old discussion. When small children ask, "Where do babies come from?" tell them that they grow from a tiny cell or seed in the mother's belly. When they ask, "How does the seed get there?" tell them that it is part of the most wonderful thing in the world, which they will get to hear all about when they turn eight. When they ask why they have to wait until they're eight, tell them that it is such a beautiful and important thing that they have to be old enough to understand it.

With this kind of a "basis" you are ready for any question, because you can answer the general parts and defer the specific parts. For example, if the small child says, "Why are boys and girls different? Why do boys have a penis and girls don't?" you can answer that boys and girls are beautiful in two different ways so that each will be special and attractive to the other— and that boys have penises not only to go to the bathroom but to do some other very important things, which will be part of the talk about "the most wonderful thing in the world" that they will get to have when they are eight.

### Teach Modesty by Example and Discussion

This can help give small children a sense of pride but also of protection of their bodies. Dress modestly even within the home and take opportunities to mention that our bodies are too wonderful and too special to be exposed to just anyone.

### Be Generous with Your Physical Affection

This gives children the security and commitment of touch and helps prevent the "physical-affection starvation" that can cause children, as they grow up, to look for physical attention from peers. Hug and kiss and pat. Begin these habits with tiny babies and continue them throughout the preschool years.

## Methods for Elementary School Age

### Spruce Up Your Own Knowledge and Understanding of the Reproductive Process

Make sure you can answer questions accurately and give yourself much-needed confidence in initiating and teaching your children about their bodies.

Go to the library or the bookstore and do a little reviewing of the terms and processes that you would like to be able to explain simply and clearly to your children.

## The Age-Eight Discussion

Use this discussion to establish a foundation for a clear and positive understanding of sex and a commitment to fidelity and chastity by your children. Follow the pattern outlined in the opening "story" of this chapter. Get one or more picture books that you feel comfortable with. Cover at least the following points:

- Names of body parts
- The natural attraction of men and women
- Sexual intercourse as a method of expression of love and commitment
- The process by which sperm fertilizes an egg and an embryo develops
- The fact that sex is beautiful and wonderful first because it starts new babies and second because it is a way a man and woman say they love each other (like a hug or a kiss, only so much deeper and more special that it should be saved and done only by a husband and wife).

Be sure you explain to your child that he will hear some kids talking about sex as if it were dirty or silly, but that is just because they don't understand it the way your child does now. Their parents may not have told them yet what you have told your child.

Also be sure to encourage questions, to ask the child if he understands, to tell him he can ask everything he wants to, at any time!

---

When our first son, Josh, turned eight, we took him on his special "mommy-daddy date" to tell him about "the most wonderful thing on earth," just as we had done with each of his two older sisters at the same age. We had to go early one evening because there was a Cub Scout and parents' dinner later that evening.

The girls had responded very quietly to our talks with them. They understood. They were very interested, and they have viewed sex very positively and openly ever since.

Josh's reaction was far more dramatic. Perhaps partly because of his acute interest in nature and science, he was enthralled by what we told him. "Wow," he kept saying, "That is *amazing.*"

We were amused by his reaction and his questions, which might have been difficult or embarrassing except that they were so candid and spontaneous. "How do chickens do it, Dad?" "How do those little sperms swim that far when they're so little?" "Was *that* what those two cats were doing at the park?"

The most dangerous part of the evening was the Cub Scout dinner. We were so rushed to get there that our talk never got to the part about privacy and only talking about these things in our own home. To Josh the earlier discussion was far more interesting than the Cub Scout dinner, so we spent the whole evening trying to change the subject as Josh kept bringing up things that we hoped the other people at the table didn't understand: "How long before a baby cat is ready to come out?" "You'd think the chicken would fall off of the other one—how does he keep his balance?" and so on.

It was a long evening!   **—Richard**

## Follow-up Discussions

Reinforce the knowledge you have passed on and your positive and "wonderful" interpretation of it. After the age-eight discussion (especially in the weeks and months following it), make opportunities for follow-up. As you tuck a child in bed, lie or sit down by him and recall the special time you had with him when he turned eight and ask if he has any questions.

As children get older, talk about puberty. Tell them what to expect (physical changes, emotional changes, and moodiness, "wet dreams" in the case of boys). Try to remember experiences from your own puberty—how you felt when certain things happened, and so on.

### The "What a Baby Needs to Grow" Game

This can help elementary, prepubescent children begin to think of sex as the important and beautiful way that children and families get *started*. Prepare the game by getting some blocks or "checkers" or anything that you can "stack up." Tape small labels to each block or checker that say:

Daddy's sperm
Mommy's egg
Food
People to teach him and help him
Clothes
Parents to love him
A warm home where he feels happy
Examples in his house of how to be a grown-up.

Without letting the children see the labels, ask them what things are required to "make and grow a baby." Give hints as necessary for children to guess the things on your blocks. Stack them up as they "get them."

As you play the game and as you finish it, ask questions like, "Do all children have this one? Do a man and woman have to be married to give this one? Do people have to love a child in order to give this one?" and so on. Use your questions and use the game to point out that it takes a *lot* to "grow a child," that the sexual act that starts a child is only the first step, and that a child who doesn't have the other steps doesn't have much of a chance. Help children see that sex should not happen between people who do not intend to provide each of the other things it takes to grow a child.

## Discussions of Movies, TV Shows, and so on

These discussions can help older elementary-age children begin to sense that sex is much more beautiful and pleasurable when it is part of real love and commitment than when it is mere experimentation or self-gratification. Watch for an opportunity (which may come through a TV show or movie) to point out that there are probably six broad reasons that a man and woman or a boy and girl would sleep together:

**1.** Experimentation (to try out sex, to see how it feels).

**2.** Self-gratification (a person does it because he wants pleasure for himself).

**3.** Ego (a person does it to prove that he can).

**4.** Acceptance (a person does it to "be like everyone else" or to keep the other person from dropping or rejecting him or her).

**5.** Love (a person does it because he loves the other person and wants to give pleasure).

**6.** Love and commitment (a person does it because it is a way of showing not only love but commitment and trust and tenderness to his or her partner).

Point out that the first five reasons are not good ones because they run a great risk of *hurting* others or hurting self. Something as intimate as sex, when it is done for one of the first four reasons, is almost sure to leave at least one of the parties feeling guilty, or used, or selfish. And, of course, if a pregnancy is started or a disease spread, the physical and emotional hurts get deeper and more complex. Even the fifth reason can be a source of hurt (sometimes the worst hurt of all) because bonds and feelings are formed that are broken without commitment.

## Methods for Adolescents

### The Mortar Metaphor

This comparison can help adolescents understand the importance of fidelity in marriage. Look for a quiet, private time (perhaps while traveling in a car or during a peaceful moment at bedtime) and relate the following comparison:

It takes many elements to build a house—the bricks, the boards, the shingles, the windows, the doors, and so on. One key element is the mortar, which holds the walls together and keeps everything in place. Similarly it takes many qualities to build a happy, unified family. It takes caring and helping and patience along with financial and emotional support. In a way the thing that "sticks" a family together and gives security and confidence to the parents and the children is the sexual fidelity of the mother and father. If either parent "cheats" on the other, it causes tremendous emotional strain. One parent feels guilty and secretive. The other feels disgraced and discarded. Even if the parents don't separate or divorce, much of the feeling and commitment is gone, and the family, like a house without mortar, can begin to break apart.

## The Horse-and-Bridle Metaphor

This can help adolescents view sex positively and at the same time recognize its *force* and the need for self-control. Find another quiet moment (like the first metaphor, this one is interesting and thought-provoking enough that your child will not feel preached to) and have a discussion with your adolescent along the following lines:

What is the purpose of a bridle for a horse? (To control the horse, to make it do what we wish it to.)

Is there any other more *complete* way to control a horse? (Tie it up, hobble it, *shoot* it.)

What's undesirable about these other ways? (They take the pleasure and purpose out of owning a horse in the first place.)

Why worry about controlling the horse? (It can run away with you; it can hurt you.)

Now, here's a tough question. What is similar about the horse and about our sexual desires and drives? (Both are very strong; both can be much stronger than we are.)

Why do we need to control our sexual appetites? (They can run away with us and hurt us or hurt other people.)

Are these desires evil or bad, then? (No, just as the horse isn't bad; they are wonderful and beautiful.)

So how could we completely control them?

(Take vows of celibacy; try to deny them or overcome them.)

Why not do that? (Because sexual desire is
good and right and natural, even though it can
be dangerous.)

So what to do? ("Bridle" it.)

How? (By deciding in advance that we will
put limits on ourselves, that we'll be true and
faithful in marriage and save the deepest forms
of physical affection for the commitment of
marriage.)

### Discussion: "The Cause, the Dangers, and the Solution"

This can give adolescents a clear understanding of
why most early sexual promiscuity occurs and a practical, workable formula for avoiding it. Before an adolescent or teenager reaches the age where you will allow
him or her to date, hold a discussion along the following
sequence of points (emphasize appropriate points for
boys or for girls accordingly):

Review the reason for the desirability for sexual abstinence prior to marriage (physical reasons—AIDS,
etc.; emotional reasons—the hurt and insecurity that can
be caused; social reasons—the desirability of a conserv-
ative rather than a "loose" reputation; mental reasons—
early sexual relationships interfere with one's ability to
focus on academic and other mental pursuits; and religious reasons—if these are important to you.

Explain that studies have been done that show that
most boys who become involved in teenage sex most
often do so for *ego* reasons (to prove their manhood, to
exploit someone, to show they can do it, to brag to their
peers), whereas most girls do so for *emotional* reasons

(desire to be accepted or not be rejected, for warmth, security, etc.). Ask if either is a good reason. Talk about any examples or "cases" that you are familiar with.

Point out that the logic most often used by boys in trying to persuade a girl to go beyond what she feels is right (and sometimes vice versa, girl persuading boy) usually takes one of two basic forms: (a) If you love me, you'll have sex with me; and (b) all the other guys I know have girlfriends who *will*.

Ask what is wrong with this logic. (Love means to respect what the other person thinks is right, not to try to manipulate them. Everyone else *doesn't* do it, and even if they did, the "everyone else" notion is a poor reason to do anything.)

Mention that there is a short, almost corny little saying that nevertheless makes a very true point about a girl (or a boy) who uses her (or his) body to attract the opposite sex. The saying is, "It works fast, but doesn't last." When we use our personality, our humor, and our real selves to attract dates and friends of the opposite sex, it "works more slowly but lasts much longer."

If (for all the reasons we have discussed) we really want to avoid too-early, or casual, or premarital sex, there is only one reliable way to do so. It is to think through possible situations we may find ourselves in and mentally rehearse exactly what we still do when that situation happens.

Describe to your adolescent, in detailed and real terms, some situations he may find himself in (alone, dark, aroused, attracted, etc., only don't just suggest adjectives—describe a real scenario). Then ask him what he would say and do. Have him be specific and think through and rehearse his actions mentally. ("I would sit up and say, 'I'm going home now'; put my car key in the ignition, start the engine; etc.")

Explain that this kind of mental rehearsal will make it much easier to do what you have decided when the time comes.

### Delay Single Dating Until a Reasonable Age

This gives adolescents time to reach a level of mental and emotional maturity that gives them a chance of handling and controlling physical and ego-centered desires. Preteen and early-teen single dating is at best rather senseless and pointless and at worst the beginning of bad choices that affect their happiness and security for the rest of their life. The early adolescent and early teen years should be times of group fun and nonpressured, noncommitted activity. Fifteen or even sixteen is not too old an age to begin single dating. Decide on limits for your own family and discuss them thoroughly with your children so they will know that they come not from lack of trust but from love and logic.

---

Sometimes the best advice we give our children (or the times we get through to them most clearly) comes when we just say what we think and catch them off guard.

A friend of mine told me of an incident when his sixteen-year-old daughter had come in late from a date, woke him (her father) up, and said, "Daddy, Rob and I want to go steady."

"You mean only date each other?" my friend said groggily.

"Yes, Dad."

Deciding it was way too late to deal with the issue that night, my friend rolled over, buried his head back in his pillow, and mumbled, "I don't know why you'd want to end your relationship. That's what going steady always does!"

Apparently his daughter thought about that, because the next morning she announced that she'd changed her mind.   —**Richard**

### Offer Physical Affection in Family Settings—Particularly Before Dates

This will increase adolescents' feelings of security and reduce their needs for physical stimulation from dating partners. Take the opportunity to give adolescents a warm hug or embrace as they leave for a date. Tell them verbally that you love, respect, and trust them. The physical hug often implants and reinforces a sense of physical security that lessens the need for physical contact on the date.

### The Verbal Game: "What Helps, What Hurts?"

This exercise helps review and put in perspective many of the principles of this chapter. Bring up various situations where sexual activity can take place (in marriage, in early dating, living together outside of marriage, in one-night stands, etc.) and ask, for each situation, "Who is helped by this? Who is or could be hurt by this?" Let the discussion flow and find opportunities to say what you think needs to be said.

### Discussion of *Immoral* and *Amoral*

This will help your children be more sensitive to and more aware of the dangers of amoral messages in music and media.

At an appropriate time discuss the differences in the definitions of the words *immoral* and *amoral*. Explain that *immoral* usually refers to the breaking of laws or the violation of values; it is wrong and it is acknowledged and recognized as wrong. *Amoral,* on the other hand, means to be without reference to right or wrong—not even to deal with the question of right or wrong.

Explain that evil or overt wrongdoing—in media or in real life—is easy to see. But amorality—the ignoring of any question about rightness or wrongness—is very subtle. Amoral media or music *portrays* acts that violate fidelity or other "rightness" in flippant or lighthearted ways, ignoring the consequences or guilt or hurt that might result.

Give examples.

Decide as a family to watch for amorality and to be able to identify it and discuss it together.

# Values
## of Giving

# Loyalty
# and Dependability

*Loyalty to family, to employers, to country, church, schools, and other organizations and institutions to which commitments are made. Support, service, contribution. Reliability and consistency in doing what you say you will do.*

———

Our two adolescent daughters learned and then put into practice a simple lesson on loyalty one week. They had planned a surprise farewell party in our home for one of their friends who was moving out of the area with her family. On the day of the party three of the girls who had accepted invitations called and, with very flimsy excuses, said they wouldn't be able to come. Our girls, who had decorated and planned for the party for some time, were first disappointed, then a little angry. "They just had something better come up," one daughter complained. "Now we won't have enough people to play some of the games." "It's inconsiderate," said the other daughter. "In fact it's rude and it's *disloyal* and *undependable.*"

Later that week *they* got invited to a party—one that they very much wanted to attend. But the party was on the night of the regular meeting and rehearsal of an organization they belonged to, which was preparing for a production. There was no question about where they would have rather gone—but there also was no question about the loyal and dependable thing to do.  **—Linda**

## GENERAL GUIDELINES

*Highlight your own dependability.* Make your children aware of your own example. Parents do things every day that illustrate their loyalty to their children and that exemplify dependability in the home setting. But so many of these things are so automatic that they are seldom noticed and seldom used as visible examples of this important moral value. Instead of saying, "I'll pick you up after school," say, "I'll be there at three-thirty—you can count on it!" Instead of just going to a child's soccer game or music recital, say, "I'll be there no matter how busy I am because I want to be with you and support what you do!"

Tell children more often that you will always be there for them, that they can depend on you, that you'll be behind them in hard times. Take credit for your dependability and loyalty, because it is the best way to instill the same qualities into your children.

*Thank children and praise them for every evidence of their own dependability.* Reinforce the value and show them how often it can be used. Thank your children when they are on time for dinner or when they support or help a smaller brother or sister. Praise them when they finish an assignment or task. Work hard this month at never taking for granted *any* act or evidence of dependability or loyalty.

## Methods for Preschoolers

### Lassie's Story

Use the following story to introduce the terms *loyalty* and *dependability* to small children; enhance and embellish the simplified story with your own goals:

Billy lived on a big farm with lots of space, so his parents let him have a dog. He called his dog Lassie. Whenever Billy called Lassie's name, the dog would come, and whenever Billy held out his hand, Lassie would put up his paw for a shake. You could *depend* on Lassie to do these things. Lassie was a *dependable* dog.

Almost everywhere Billy went, Lassie followed. At night Lassie slept at the bottom of Billy's bed. If Billy ever got in any trouble, Lassie was there to help. Lassie was *loyal* because he cared about Billy and was always there when he needed him.

One day Billy wandered into a field where a big bull lived. The bull charged toward Billy. Billy called as loud as he could for his *loyal* dog who was close by. He knew he could *depend* on him. Lassie rushed into the field and barked at the bull. The bull turned around and went back to eat his grass.

### The Pick-the-Right-Answer Game

This game can help small children who have started reading to understand and even use the words *loyal* and *dependable*.

Prepare a "windowpane" chart that shows the two words and their opposites:

| dependable | undependable |
|:---:|:---:|
| loyal | disloyal |

Explain that you are going to tell a little story about several different people and you want the child to point to the word on the chart that describes how the person is acting or behaving.

- Timmy's dad asked him if he would stack up some bricks in the garage. Timmy said he would, but he forgot and didn't do it. *(Undependable.)*
- Janet's school class planned to have a car wash in the school parking lot to raise money. Those who could were asked to come and help, but no one had to come. Janet came and brought some towels and a bucket. *(Loyal—to her school.)*
- Crissy's family job was to set the table each night for dinner. She almost always remembered to do it without her mother reminding her. *(Dependable.)*
- Tammy was with two girls on the bus one day when one of the girls said some bad things that weren't true about Tammy's best friend, Jill.

Tammy didn't say anything. (*Disloyal*—to her friend.)

- Jason's little brother had a Little League game one night. Jason had a lot of homework, but he worked hard at it until game time and then went to cheer for his brother. (*Loyal*—to his brother.)
- The elderly widow who lived next door to Mary had a favorite plant that needed watering every day. She asked Mary if she would water it for a week while she was on vacation. Mary did it for four days, but then she forgot. *(Undependable.)*
- Alice always thought about the Pledge of Allegiance when her class said it. She felt proud to be an American. (*Loyal*—to her country.)

---

Richard and I host a weekly national cable-TV show on families and parenting.* Sometimes our children tune in at home. When we first began the show, this "loyal watching" was almost our undoing.

I remember on the second or third show we did, we had a question from a woman in the studio audience about how to stop her two boys from fighting so much. In answering her, I mentioned a fight that had occurred in our house the week before in which Talmadge had hit Noah.

When we got home that evening, the children were irate. "Mom! It wasn't Talmadge that hit Noah. It was *Josh*. And it happened Wednesday, not Tuesday, and the reason he hit him wasn't because he left the gerbil cage open; it was because he took the gerbil out and it got mixed up with one of his gerbils and . . ."

Ever since, we've been much more careful about the accuracy of any story we relate—because we know that several *loyal* little critics are listening to our every word.   —**Linda**

*The Eyres' show, *Families are Forever,* is broadcast on the VISN cable network and listed in *TV Guides* as "Families."

---

### Family Traditions, Mottoes, Slogans, and so on

These can help small children feel the security of belonging to a strong family, to an institution for which they can feel loyalty. Develop a simple family slogan and motto and say them together every day for a while. Then perhaps once a week. Create simple family traditions (often built around holidays or birthdays) that you repeat year after year. Have one ongoing family tradition of supporting other family members in their activities. (Attend games, performances, etc.)

### Ask Small Children to Do Things Instead of Telling Them

You'll obtain their *answer,* which you can use to teach dependability. When children are told to do something, they can learn and practice only the principle of obedience. But when small children are asked to do something in a firm but respectful way, they can learn both obedience and dependability.

Children actually say no, complain, and make excuses more when they are told than when they are asked. Use the word *please,* and let them know that you expect a yes. That yes then becomes a commitment to which you can tie the principle of dependability . . . of *doing* what you say you will do.

### "Starting Over"

Give your children second chances to be dependable. When small children fail to do something they've said they will do, say, "Let's start over and do this right. Let's be dependable. Let's pretend I've never asked you to do that. Now I'm going to ask you—and let's see what you do."

## Methods for Elementary School Age

### The Synonyms and Antonyms Game

This game will help late elementary school or early-adolescent children be clear in their understanding of both words. Simply ask, "What are some synonyms or close synonyms for *dependability?*" (*Reliability, trustworthiness, consistency, predictability*, etc.) "For *loyalty?*" (*To stand up for, to be part of, to be true to.*) "What are some antonyms or near antonyms for *dependable?*" (*Can't be counted on, unpredictable.*) "For *loyal?*" (*Uncommitted, traitor, spy, out for oneself.*) Then discuss how dependability helps people and how its opposites hurt people.

### Discussion

Help your children see the concepts more clearly and become comfortable thinking about them. Ask them *what* or *who* they could be loyal to (country, church, school, employer, friends, family, etc.). Then ask them *who* should be able to depend on them (parents, teachers, friends, employers, etc.).

### The True-and-False-Loyalty Discussion

This is a good way to help children see the difference between loyalty and "not ratting." Explain that some children get the idea that loyalty to friends means "not telling on them" or "keeping quiet" or even lying to protect them. This is "*false* loyalty." Explain that if someone has done something wrong, a truly loyal friend would try to get him to admit it, and if that didn't work, he would tell someone. If neither happens, the friend will probably keep doing wrong and get in more serious trouble.

## Stories

These can help children feel and live situations of loyalty and dependability vicariously. Elementary-age children are the easiest age to make up stories for. This month tell them a bedtime story or two (out of your own mind) about dependability or loyalty. Example topics: A spy story—someone who was a disloyal traitor. A sports story—maybe a member of a relay team who was tired after his individual event but still ran the relay because he was loyal to his team. A harvest story—a child who watered his garden consistently and dependably and was rewarded with a good harvest.

## Metaphor of Constructing a Building

This can help children understand that "doing one's part" is a key part of loyalty. Ask children to imagine that there were 100 people who wanted to build a brick wall and that the wall would need 10,000 bricks. How many bricks would each person have to put up if they all helped? (100) How many bricks would each person have to put up if only 10 helped? (1,000) Make the point that when people are *loyal,* everything is more pleasant and more fair.

## Dependability and Loyalty Awards

Recognize children who do well at being dependable and loyal. Have Dependability and Loyalty awards. As usual with the awards, pick a Sunday dinner (or whatever time you choose) and ask, "Who had an experience this past week in which they were loyal?" Do the same with dependability. Give liberal encouragement and praise. Also give your own personal examples and enter the competition yourself.

———

A friend of ours has always been particularly loyal to and supportive of his children. One of his boys was good enough to make the community youth football team, but not good enough to play very much. As he spent most of the season on the bench, his father was always in the stands or on the sidelines, rarely missing a game.

One day as they drove home after another game in which the boy had not played, the son said to the father, "Dad, you don't have to keep coming—I hardly ever get to play anyway."

The father responded, "Son, do you think I come to the games just to see you play? I come because I want to be *with* you. It doesn't matter to me how much you play. If you are on the bench, I still want to be there giving you my support."  **—Richard**

———

## Variable Rewards

Reward children for dependability—and increase that reward when dependability comes without reminders. In connection with assigning children family jobs and attaching financial rewards to them, try telling them that there are two levels of rewards and they can choose (in advance) the one they want. The highest level (most money) is for doing their job without being asked or reminded. The risk is that they will forget and thus get nothing. The second level offers less money, but with it you will remind them if they forget. Let them choose whichever "scheme" they wish for each week.

## Methods for Adolescents

### The Three-Part Discussion

This will expand adolescents' understanding and build their desire for dependability and loyalty.

- Go through the "Synonyms and Antonyms Game" and the discussion from page 151 to fix definitions in children's minds.
- Then ask, "What is the difference between dependability and loyalty?" While they have many similar and overlapping aspects, *dependability* is especially concerned with doing what one says he will do—keeping commitments and being reliable. *Loyalty* includes being dependable but also implies support, service, and contribution to the person or thing to which loyalty is given.
- Cautions on both: Ask what one has to be careful about in striving to live by these two principles. *Dependability:* Be careful not to make commitments you can't keep . . . or to make more (too many) commitments than you can keep. Part of being dependable is to carefully choose commitments and then make them totally. *Loyalty:* First, be careful and cautious about giving loyalty. Don't give loyalty to too many things. Save deepest loyalty for deepest loves. Second, *never* confuse loyalty with "not ratting on someone." (See "True and False Loyalty Discussion" on page 151.

### Lists

These help children pinpoint who and what they want to be loyal to and what things they want to be dependable on. Work together with the children on forming a loyalty list (family members, school, church, friends, etc.) and a dependability list (family job, school assignments, music practice, etc.).

## Pass It On

Case studies can help adolescents see the far-reaching effects of dependability. For example, Jim has won a part in the church play and committed himself to be at practices on Tuesday and Thursday nights. He is studying with a friend, loses track of time, and misses a key practice. Who is affected? (Others in the play, who can't rehearse their lines without his. The director, who has to shift things around. Ultimately the audience who may see a less professional play.) Think of other examples.

## Discussion of True Friendship

Summarize the value of dependability and loyalty. Ask adolescents what they think is the most important and valuable quality in a friend. Challenge them to think of any more important or more crucial factor than loyalty and dependability.

*Month 8:*

# Respect

*Respect for life, for property, for parents, for elders, for nature, and for the beliefs and rights of others. Courtesy, politeness, and manners. Self-respect and the avoidance of self-criticism.*

---

I remember an article in a newspaper on little Prince William, the then five-year-old son of Prince Charles and Lady Diana of England, that pointed out that although the little fellow was independent and a bit rambunctious, he was also extremely polite and respectful. He always opened doors for ladies, addressed men as "sir," and said "please" and "thank you." His parents, the article said, had instructed the royal nanny to put high priority on teaching him to be a "respectful young gentleman."

"Now, that's what we need," I thought to myself (not the nanny—although that need had also occurred to me)—"a little more *respect*." I tore out the article and took it up with the kids that evening at dinner, explaining very firmly that from now on we were going to have better manners and more respect.

I asked them what they thought *respect* meant and got the answers I wanted. "Being polite," "being courteous," "helping other people."

Then I got an answer far better than what I thought I wanted—far better than the answer I had in my own mind. It came from an adolescent daughter, who said, "I think it's nice that Prince William calls people 'sir' and I think manners are important, but respect isn't just using the right words and being well trained. *Respect* means really caring about how people feel." **—Linda**

---

The importance of and basic necessity for respect are self-evident. Respect is the basis and foundation (and often the motivation) for several of the other basic values of life. Children who learn both to implement and to understand the principle of respect will be better members of society, better friends, and better leaders.

The teaching of respect is an interesting and somewhat difficult proposition. The main thing to remember is that respect isn't *given* consistently unless it is *received*. We need first to respect our children (in terms of how we speak to them and how we treat them) and then to absolutely demand that they show repsect for us in return. The respect they *receive* in the home will be the basis for their own self-respect; and the respect they learn to *show* in the home (to family members) will be the foundation on which to build respect for others outside the home.

## GENERAL GUIDELINES

*Extend respect and then expect respect.* Create the proper climate for respect in your own home. We often speak to and deal with our children with less respect than we show to strangers. We treat them as though they have no rights and deserve no explanations. We say "because I said so" and we give them no benefit of the doubt and assume they are guilty until proven innocent.

We need to change this, even if it requires imagining that they are strangers and speaking to them accordingly. Use the words "please" and "thank you" more. *Ask* them whenever possible instead of telling them. Ask for their advice or input on things. Respect their opinions.

Once we make this effort, we are in a position to expect (even demand) respect in return. Make it clear that respect includes tone of voice as well as manners. This expectation must be consistent and repetitive. Simply do not allow disrespect in your home.

*Give plenty of praise and recognition.* Reinforce respectful behavior and encourage its repetition. Make up your mind to watch for opportunities to praise courtesy and politeness during the month. Catch them doing something right and make a big deal of it. Praise them in front of other family members—and then try to remember to praise them privately, one on one, later the same day.

*Give them a chance to correct themselves by saying "Let's start over."* This is a good method to correct disrespectful behavior in a positive way. Establish the pattern (and the habit, in connection with consistently not allowing disrespect in the home) of saying, "Let's start over." When a disrespectful answer is given, when someone fails to say "please" or "thank you," say "Let's start over." Then repeat the situation, letting the child do it right. Do this with children of all ages. And when necessary, say, "Let's start over" for yourself and then repeat your own statement or behavior in a more respectful way.

*Teach by your own examples.* Show respectful behavior. As always, example is the best teacher. During this month be ever-conscious of respect. Let your children see and hear you being concerned for the property and rights of others, assisting the elderly, caring for nature, being polite in all situations and showing self-respect in terms of how you look and how you speak of yourself.

## Methods for Preschoolers

### The Definitions Game

Use this game to get *respect* into the vocabulary of small children so that both you and they can *use* the word. Tell them that *respect* means "acting nice and talking nice and minding." Then tell them about Mikey. Ask them whether he was showing respect after each sentence.

- Mikey's mom asked him to clean up his room and he yelled, "I don't want to!" *(No.)*
- He picked all the flowers out of his neighbor's garden. *(No.)*
- He said, "Please, may I be excused?" *(Yes.)*
- He looked his grandpa in the eye and said, "Fine, sir," when Grandpa said, "How are you?" *(Yes.)*
- He left his friend's toy out in the rain. *(No.)*
- When he couldn't put the puzzle together, he said, "I'm just stupid." *(No.)*

### The Role-Playing Game

This game gives small children some grasp of *why* respect should be shown. *You* play the role of the child and let the child play the other roles. Act each out. Then ask, "How does that make you feel?"

- Child says, "Thank you very much" when Grandpa gives him some candy.
- Grass begins to die (child plays grass) because child stomps on it instead of walking on sidewalk.
- Children are noisy in a class while teacher is trying to teach.
- Child pushes himself in front of an older lady at the checkout stand in the grocery store.
- Child holds his mother's chair as they sit down to eat and then says, "Thanks for this nice dinner, Mom."
- Child is noisy in church and the lady next to him can't hear the service.
- Child keeps interrupting his mother while she is trying to talk to a friend who has stopped by.

———

One summer we were fortunate enough to take all of the children on a trip to the Grand Canyon and some of the natural wonders of the Southwest. As we stood on one of the vistas and gazed at the incredible majesty of canyon and rock, our eight-year-old said, "You know, Mom, kids use the word *awesome* a lot—but *this,* now this really *is* awesome!"

We sat on that rocky point for quite a while talking about the earth's majesty and about the respect we should have for the earth, for nature, and for the forces that created them.   **—Linda**

———

### The Red-Marks-and-Black-Marks Chart

This exercise can help little children "keep track" and count incidents of respect and disrespect. Prepare a simple chart with the child's (or children's) name(s) on it. Explain that whenever he does something that shows disrespect (yells at Mom, interrupts, demands something without saying please, etc.), he will get a black mark. Whenever he is polite or uses good manners, he gets a red mark. Divide the chart by days and tell the child to see if he can get more red marks than black each day.

### "Magic" Words

This can help young children *want* to use simple etiquette and politeness. Play a game where you "catch" the children and they say "abracadabra" to make you let them go. Then ask them if they want to learn some more magic words. Explain that *please* will often cause people to do things; *thank you* will help others feel happy inside; *excuse me* will help make friends, keep people calm, and so on.

## Methods for Elementary School Age

### Expand the "Definitions Game"

This can help children see that lack of respect *hurts* someone or something. Ask the questions from the Definitions Game for preschoolers (page 159). Follow each question with, "Who does that show disrespect for? And how does the disrespect make that person feel?"

### The "Who and How" Chart

This helps children *plan* to be respectful. Set up a chart, perhaps on a large poster board, looking something like the one on page 163.

Using the left-hand column, ask children to list the categories of people and things that deserve respect. As you list them one at a time, discuss *how* respect for that person or thing can be effectively given. (E.g., for "Mother": by "answering respectfully," "by obeying her," "showing appreciation for what she does," "opening door," "holding her chair," etc. For "Nature": by "preserving and protecting," "clearing and cultivating," etc. For "Self": by "avoiding self-criticism," "thinking about positive attributes," etc.) Keep the list building as long as you can keep children's interest.

### "Election" of Family Traditions of Courtesy

This is a good way to help develop *habits* of respect. In a family home evening or around the dinner table, have a "vote" to pick three family traditions of politeness. Open the meeting to "nominations," which could be anything from opening doors for people to looking people in the eye to saying thank you. Keep nominations open until you have at least six things on a list. Discuss their relative importance and vote on them. Each family member has three votes. Make up a chart showing the three winners, label it "Family Traditions" and put it up in a visible place.

### Family Nontraditions—Deciding Together What Not to Do

This will focus the weight of family agreement on disrespectful acts. Have a similar "nominating and vote"

| RESPECT CHART | |
|---|---|
| **WHO** | **HOW** |
| Mother | obey her<br>talk respectfully |
| Nature | |
| Self | |
| Etc. | |

night to pick the three worst and most disrespectful kinds of behavior. Nominees could include crude language or swearing, yelling at parents, crowding in line, and so on. After you have selected the "three worst," see what the children would propose as punishment for those who do them (e.g., going to their room for yelling at their parents).

### Story of a Great Man's Respect for His Wife

Try to give your children a memorable *example* of respect. As the ninety-year-old religious leader got out of his car (driven by a chauffeur) to go into church, he needed help to climb out and to stand. Still, with a helper on each elbow, he insisted on walking around the car to open the door for his wife, also ninety years old, and to offer her his hand as she got out. Many of those who watched were impressed and overcome to the point of tears.

## Methods for Adolescents

### Discussion: "Why respect, why manners?"

Get your older children thinking about the practicality and reasoning around the habits of politeness. Play devil's advocate. Say, "Aren't manners a little silly? Using little unnecessary words, opening doors for people who can open them themselves, standing up to greet people. Why do formal, traditional things like this anyway?" Challenge the kids to defend politeness.

### Discussion of the Application of Childhood Manners to Adulthood

Help adolescents understand that the manners and simple lessons of respect that they learned as children apply equally to adults. Read out loud together the following quote from the Reverend Robert Fulghum:

> Most of what I really need to know about how to live and what to do and how to be I learned in kindergarten. . . . These are the things I learned: Share everything. Play fair. Don't hit people. . . . clean up your own mess. Don't take things that aren't yours. Say you're sorry when you hurt somebody.

Discuss the statement. Do the simple things we learned in kindergarten still apply? Would the world be a better place if adults all continued to practice and implement these simple lessons? And so on.

### Insult List

Point out the damage and danger of talking negatively to and about *yourself*. This teaches the practice of self-respect. Take a blank sheet of paper and ask kids to think about names they have called themselves or insults they have said or thought about themselves. Approach it lightheartedly and with a little humor. Get it started by listing some things you have called yourself ("stupid," "jerk," "klutz," "forgetful boob," "idiot") or sarcastic things you have said to yourself ("Oh, that's really nice," "Great shot, dummy," etc.).

When you have a substantial list, turn serious and say, "How would you feel if a friend or peer said those things to you?" Point out that deep down in our sub-conscious our own self-criticism is probably at least as harmful as the same words coming from someone else.

———

One advantage (or one penalty, according to how you look at it) of a large family like ours is that there seems to be a personality of virtually every type!

Our Jonah, to both his credit and his detriment, is a perfectionist. This quality causes him to be motivated and self-reliant, but it also causes him to worry and to be highly self-critical. From the time that he was a small preschooler, I can recall him murmuring to himself about how slow he was, how no one would like what he'd done, how badly he had messed something up.

One week I tried to make a note of every negative or critical thing I heard him say about himself. By the end of the week I had about a dozen. I wrote them on a list and sat down with nine-year-old Jonah. "Son, here is a list of some names I heard a person call someone. Pretty bad, aren't they? What do you think a person should do if someone called him these names?"

"I don't know—tell him to stop, I guess."

"Right!" I said. "I agree. He should tell the person to stop. Now, guess who this person was and guess who he was calling by these names?"

After a couple of hints Jonah guessed that he was both the person calling the names and the person being called the names.

We went on to discuss the importance of showing respect for self.

—Richard

———

## Case Study

Telling this story can help adolescents see that their happiness is connected both to the respect they receive and to the respect they give:

A family went to live in a foreign country for a year while the father completed a research project. The two teenagers, partly because they were very homesick, were critical and disrespectful of everything. They hated the narrow roads, the different fashions, the wet weather, the strange shops. They criticized and complained to each other and to anyone who would listen. Their parents kept telling them to grow up, to quit being so silly, to shut up if they couldn't think of anything nice to say.

Why were the two teenagers so unhappy? (They weren't giving respect—respect leads to positive attitudes and feelings. And they weren't receiving respect—their parents belittled their feelings instead of trying to understand.)

### The "What Does It Lead To?" Game

This game can help adolescent and late-elementary-age children see the ramifications of respect and of its opposite. Do an arrow diagram on a chart or blackboard. Start with *respect* and *rudeness* and then let the children think of words that they lead to.

For example:

Rudeness → selfishness → enemies → anger
Respect → kindness → friendliness → understanding

*Month 9:*

# Love

Individual and personal caring that goes both beneath and beyond loyalty and respect. Love for friends, neighbors, even adversaries. And a prioritized, lifelong commitment of love for family.

───────

Our youngest child is named Charity. We like the sound of the word as well as its definition of "pure love." A few weeks before her first birthday we were trying to generate a discussion of love with our older children around the dinner table. What is love? What causes us to feel it for others? And why are some people so much easier to feel it for than others?

Hard questions; especially for children. No—maybe especially hard for adults and easier for children. The discussion went beyond what we had hoped. We found ourselves learning instead of teaching. We talked about love meaning *caring* and about how we love those who love us and do things for us. Then our eleven-year-old daughter brought up the illustration of baby Charity. "She doesn't do things for us, we do everything for her, and just think how much we all love Charity!"

"Well, she does love us," said the seven-year-old, "you can tell that by how she looks at you."

"And she never tells you to be different," said our nine-year-old son, "she just seems to like you no matter what."   **—Richard**

What are the messages?

First, we learn to love by serving others.

Second, we learn to love by being loved unconditionally.

The principle: We may not always love those who serve us. Their love, depending on how it is given, can spoil us, or intimidate us, or even antagonize us. But unconditional, understanding, fully accepting love warms us without reservation and brings about our reciprocal love. And while we may not necessarily love those who serve us, we *will* love those whom we serve.

Thus, all of the methods in this chapter boil down to giving children unconditional love and giving them opportunities to serve.

## GENERAL GUIDELINES

*Clearly separate dissatisfaction with behavior from love of child.* Assure and reassure your children of your unconditional love for them. At every instance of discipline or correction reiterate that it is what the child *did* that you do not like and that your love for the child cannot be altered by anything. Mention this frequently to children of all ages and back it up with a hug and physical affection. Say, "James, I was really upset when you were two hours late getting home from school and didn't call me, and you deserve the penalty you're getting, but I want to remind you that it's what you *did* that I'm not so wild about. I still love *you* as much as ever. I always do and always will!"

*Develop a service orientation.* You and your children can learn collectively to love through serving. Any kind of service project is a "petri dish" for growing love. Look for charitable services that can be rendered as a family and that can involve your children. These can range from "Sub-for-Santa" charity programs at Christmastime to clean-up, fix-up projects in summer to helping needy people at any time of year.

---

Our son Josh was trying to decide on his "Eagle project" for Scouts. It was midwinter and his Scout master mentioned that the local shelter was now providing beds for over two hundred helpless men. Josh decided to organize a big chili dinner for them. He recruited the other Scouts (actually the other Scouts' mothers) to make big pots of chili. He got rolls and fruit and punch donated by various individuals and let his brothers and sisters help out with the preparations. When the big night came, he watched with pride as the children served up chili in Styrofoam bowls to appreciative down-and-out men, who thanked them profusely and sat on their cots to eat. We watched the kids hand out rolls and carrots and apples and doughnuts. We watched the interactions and the looks of pity, of appreciation, of love. One man said he had once been an Eagle Scout himself and asked Josh if he could attend the Court of Honor when Josh got his Eagle. On the way home that night and for days thereafter, the kids talked about little else.

And in their words were the insights of compassion and the tones of love for those they had served.   **—Linda**

_____

*Provide and Allow for Apology and "Repentance"* This helps show children that you place love and improvement over punishment and penalty. Too often, well-meaning parents adopt an almost Gestapo-like mentality of "justice" and retribution. "Break a law, get a punishment."

Love is better taught in settings where "repentance" or restitution is an alternative to punishment.

Teach children that when they make a mistake, or lose their temper, or break a family law, they can often avoid a punishment if they apologize, make restitution, and promise not to "do it again." For smaller children use the "repenting bench" mentioned earlier. When two children fight or argue, sit them on the bench and tell them that the only way to get off the bench is to say what *they* (not the other guy) did wrong, to apologize (including a hug), and to promise not to do it again. Help them to see that whenever there is a fight or argument, *both* parties have done something ("it takes two to tangle").

Praise them and show pride for any "repenting" they do. The whole process can add to the love that is expressed and felt in your home.

## Methods for Preschoolers

Teaching preschool children to love and prioritize loving themselves and their family above all other things is a wonderful gift that will stay with them throughout their lives.

### Service in the Home

One way to teach small children love is through service. If given proper instruction, even a three-year-old can set the table, put his own toys away, and help make his bed, even though these tasks are much easier to do yourself. If performing these tasks is prefaced by comments from the parents about how happy it makes them when children help, these simple tasks can be used to help the preschooler experience the joy of showing love through service.

### Secret Services

This can help young children taste the delight of anonymous giving. With your little ones, decide on something you can do for someone anonymously. It may be baking cookies and leaving a little basket of them on Daddy's pillow or on the bed of an older brother or sister. It may be leaving a bowl of fruit on the door-step of an elderly neighbor or sending a grandparent a new pair of slippers with no return address on the package.

### Bedtime Stories

Telling stories is a great way to illustrate uncondi-tional love and to help children separate your dissatis-faction with their actions from your dissatisfaction with them. Use the following ideas as guidelines and expand them into stories. Add more personal examples if desired.

- One afternoon Jamie came from playing with his friend in the open field next to his house with his shoes covered with mud. His beautiful new leather athletic shoes that his mom had bought him just the day before now looked terrible. Do you think Jamie's mother still loved him?
- Two-year-old Allison wanted to know if her big sister's favorite baby doll knew how to swim, so she put her in the toilet to find out. Do you think Allison's sister still loved her?
- Tommy found a little loose flap in the new wallpaper of Daddy's den and wondered if his tiniest truck could fit under it. It didn't quite fit and Tommy tore the wallpaper trying to get the opening a little bigger. Do you think Tommy's daddy still loved him when he found the torn wallpaper?
- Jeremy's mother told Jeremy that he couldn't go to play with his friend, Anthony, because Anthony had a cold and Jeremy's mom didn't want him to get a cold too. After Jeremy had asked to go to Anthony's again and again and his mother kept saying no and started to get angry with Jeremy for asking, Jeremy screamed, "I hate you!" and threw himself on the floor, crying and kicking. Do you think Jeremy's mother still loved him?

## Methods for Elementary School Age

### Taking Responsibility for Younger Siblings

You can teach love to this age group by giving them the privilege of helping and serving younger children.

Call the older child a tutor and tell him that the younger child is his tutee. Tell the older child that he will have the opportunity of helping that little child in many ways. He can sit next to the child at mealtimes and help him with cutting meat, pouring milk, and finishing his food. He can also be the one to hold that little child's hand at the zoo, put him to bed, read stories to him at bedtime, and generally act as the younger child's guardian angel. Attach a time limit (e.g., "You can be your little brother's tutor for one month") and offer a monetary reward, if you think it's appropriate, for his help. The older child will not only learn to love whom he serves but will also have an added appreciation for you as his parents as he helps with things you usually do.

### Pets

Pets can be a great method for teaching children to love (although many a mother has thrown her hands up in exasperation as she cleans up the "outside dog's" messes in the house time after time and finds the food and water bowl empty again). But great lessons of love as well as dependability and responsibility can be taught through teaching children to care for pets.

---

We speak with some authority (or at least with some experience) on the topic of pets.

Being foster parents to Esmeralda, a puppy; Pearl, a kitten; BaBa, a turtle; Brumbie, a cockateel; Banner, a horse; Cosette, a bunny; Geneva, a cat; Slimy, a snake; and a never-ending parade of tropical fish and gerbils, we can give endless examples of wonderful learning experiences through successes and failures, birth and deaths, regarding pets. However, the bottom line is that pets are a great tool in teaching love.   **—Linda**

_____

## Show Physical Love

Show your love openly and teach your children that overt affection and love is okay. Give hugs. Children need to feel their parents' physical love as much during their elementary-school-age years as they do as preschoolers. Whether it is as your child goes off to school, just before he pops into bed, or, as we do at our house, just after family prayer, a sincere hug is appreciated by everyone, even teenagers, whether they will openly admit it or not. Be sure to tell children verbally that you love them as well as providing hugs. A quick "love you" as they dash off with their friends will give them added security.

## Methods for Adolescents

### Set an Example of Tolerance

Teach children to accept people who are different from them by being tolerant of other lifestyles. Help them to see that "our way" of doing things is not the only way and perhaps not always the best way. Adolescents can see that there are interesting things to be learned and loved about people from all lifestyles. Also, talk with children about _why_ people are the way they are and discuss possible reasons and causes for people's observed problems.

During the month we were concentrating on love and tolerance, "Drug Awareness Week" was held at our junior high school. Several former drug addicts from all different social and economic backgrounds came and spoke to the kids. We were proud of how our seventh-grader responded when he came home and said, "Mom, they were all just really nice people who either thought they would like to have an adventure or needed to get out of the real world because their lives were in such a mess."   —Linda

### Look for Special Needs... and the Service Award.

It's important to teach children to look for those who need help.

One father taught awareness and love for others by asking his son every day, when he came home from school, "Son, did you help anyone today?" At first the son looked back at him blankly and said, "Well, no." The father just smiled and changed the subject. After being asked the same question and giving the same answer about twenty days in a row, one day the son finally said yes! and told how he had noticed a handicapped boy and helped him get to class.

As parents we need to let our children know that it is important to us that they learn to love others by looking for opportunities to help. As always, example is the best teacher and we need to share our own personal efforts to give help or service.

One of our favorite Sunday awards is the Service Award, which we give out each week at the Sunday dinner table. We ask the children to think of and relate any incident from the past week when they saw a need and were able to help. The child with the best example receives the Service Award, which consists of a little paper poster plaque that can be hung on his door for the coming week. The elementary-age children seem to love the Sunday award sessions most, although young adolescents and even older teenagers sometimes enjoy the recognition of relating experiences from their week. The award sessions, and especially this particular award, also build a special love for brothers and sisters (as when a sister who has felt contempt for a brother during the week hears that he has really tried to help someone else and thus realizes that he can't be all bad).   —**Richard**

---

### Care and Organizational Involvement

These can teach a love for self and for the community. For some adolescent boys the Scouting program is a great way to boost self-esteem and develop a love for the community. Community-service projects and various other aid and "help" organizations can provide similar opportunities for involvement.

---

For many years I have served on the board of an organization called the Community Services Council. The organization operates a food bank, and our children have had the experience of delivering food to needy people. We also developed a "sister community" relationship with a region of poor villages in drought-stricken Mali in sub-Saharan Africa, and our children now feel a certain bond of compassion with the African children whose pictures I have brought back with me.

But I think the most powerful (and certainly the most personal) experience our children have derived from this community-service organization was their relationship with Mr. Boyle. Mr. Boyle was an eighty-six-year-old who had no children, no spouse, no living relatives and lived alone in his tiny and somewhat unkempt home. One project of the council is to locate such individuals and link them up with families who will visit and befriend them. We were assigned to Mr. Boyle.

We went over every week to mow his lawn, clean his kitchen, or just to sit and chat (we should say *listen,* because the main thing Mr. Boyle needed was someone to talk to, and he had a great deal to say!) Sometimes all of our children would go, but more often just a couple of them went at a time. Whenever Mr. Boyle saw us on his doorstep, his eyes would fill with tears, and a big smile would fill his lovely old face.

After a six-month absence (when we were living abroad to finish some writing), we returned to find that Mr. Boyle's health had worsened and he had been moved to a rest home. I'm sure he misses us, but perhaps not as much as our children miss him—and miss the warmth and love that come from giving service and meeting another person's needs.   **—Richard**

## Case Studies

These can help the older adolescent realize that love sometimes involves tough decisions. Talking about case studies with teenagers can help them to sort out their own cases. At bedtime talk with your adolescents about some of the following case studies:

- Judy wants to go to a party where she knows there will be drinking and perhaps drugs. She is going with three friends, two of whom she knows are only interested in the party, not the drinking or drugs. She is trying to decide whether or not to go and how much to tell her parents about the details of the party. What do you think she should do?

- Jonathan really wants to take the car and go to a movie with a friend, but his parents are going out and will be taking the only available car. Besides that, his parents need a baby-sitter for his younger brother. Jonathan has had a really grueling week at school and really feels that he needs to relax and "escape" to the movie. What should be done?

- Nancy has more homework than she can possibly get done without staying up until two A.M. And she has to get up to get ready to go to school and do her piano practice by six A.M. the next morning. She also needs to have had enough sleep to get her through her test in math. What should she do? What should her parents do to help her?

Think of case studies from your own life or from past experience that will give you some interesting dilemmas to discuss together—dilemmas that can sometimes be solved by good communication and by parents and children being willing to give up their own interests to help each other.

The answers and solutions will be different according to the parents and the child involved, but it will be interesting to talk with your child about various possibilities before the actual situation arises. If the parent can remain open-minded and the child can be honest, the love between parent and child is bound to increase.

### If You Love Them, Tell Them

Form a parental habit of saying "I love you." It seems that teenagers are always doing things differently than we would do them. Sometimes, with all our criticism, it is hard for adolescents to remember that we love them. The best solution to their problem is to tell them that we love them, not only through the things that we do for them but by saying "I love you" as they leave for school, as they go to bed, and especially when they do something that makes you happy or proud. Think about how long it has been since you have told your adolescents that you love them. If it has been a while, it may seem difficult and awkward. Do it anyway. You may be surprised at how soon they'll be saying the same thing to you.

# Unselfishness and Sensitivity

*Becoming more extra-centered and less self-centered. Learning to feel with and for others. Empathy, tolerance, brotherhood. Sensitivity to needs in people and situations.*

Sensitivity and empathy are values of obvious importance, but they are also qualities usually associated with maturity. Can they be taught to children?

———

Our son Josh was having a sledding party for his sixth birthday. Shawni, Josh's eight-year-old sister, came along to keep her dad company and to help with the hot cider and doughnuts we planned to serve.

There were a dozen boys at the party and they were all whooping it up and having a great time. At least that's how it looked to me.

Then I observed a most amazing thing. Josh came up to the top of the hill with two of his friends, and Shawni met him there and said, "Josh, this is a great party and most of the boys are having a good time, but that boy over there (pointing) is being left out and doesn't look like he's having much fun, and the boy in the red coat at the bottom of the hill can't get his sleigh to go very well and he looks a little upset. You should go make both of them feel better."

This sensitive eight-year-old had noticed what I hadn't—that two boys weren't having as much fun as the others. Rather than being self-conscious or bored or worried about being the only girl there and older than the boys, she was *watching* them, thinking about them, and being sensitive and concerned about them.

—**Richard**

———

Some children have a natural and seemingly inherent sense of caring and sensitivity. Such cases are rather rare, however, and the self-centered "surrounded by mirrors" perspective of life is typical of most children, particularly adolescents. In fact most of the problems teenagers face (whether taking the form of rebellion or of extreme shyness and withdrawal) stem from their rather intense preoccupation with self.

Nevertheless, children can begin to learn sensitivity and unselfishness at a very young age, and they should learn it as a skill and a capacity as well as a value.

Children have difficulty empathizing and applying their own feelings to others. A child can feel crushed one day because Jimmy didn't invite him to his birthday party and the next day forget to include someone who looks lonely in the basketball game at recess. Adolescents love to borrow clothes, but many hate to lend them and often forget to return them or to "repair the damage." It takes real effort on the part of parents and sometimes a very long time for most children to realize that the world does not revolve around them, that others' feelings are crucial and that there is a great deal to be learned from giving up something they really want for the sake of someone else.

———

One day our six- and nine-year-olds decided they wanted the same chair at the same moment. It was like the immovable object meeting the irresistible force. Each child insisted that this last available chair to sit on was in precisely the right spot for him and that he had gotten there first. When the battle of the iron wills turned into shouting and crying and looked close to physical violence, I considered two alternatives: (a) spend a little time to find out who was right; or (b) send them to the "repenting bench" until each could figure out what he did wrong. In this case I decided neither would work. I said, "I'm going to watch you two and see which one is going to be a Leader for the Right [see page 00]. I think you both know the right thing to do to take care of this problem." After a fifteen-second silence, the child I would have bet on relinquished his half of the chair to the other, whose face reflected a double exposure of relief and guilt. After seeing the praise lavished on the unselfish child, the other offered the chair back to the first. If our attention hadn't been diverted by the rush to get to school, they probably could have worked up a new argument about who was the most unselfish. —**Linda**

———

## GENERAL GUIDELINES

*Praise.* Reinforce—and cause repetition of—unselfish behavior. *Heap* praise on signs or symptoms or even brief glimpses of selflessness in children of any age! Let's face it, an act of simple sharing in children—particularly small ones—is cause for genuine celebration. And it also calls for praise and recognition. When a child shares, or gives, or sees and responds to needs in another, praise him, pick him up and hug him, and point out what he's just done to anyone else who is around.

*Give responsibility.* Try to bring out your children's appreciation and empathy for the difficulties and challenges of others. A recent Harvard study pointed up an interesting connection between how much responsibility children were given and their tendencies to be altruistic and extra-centered. Apparently children who are given everything but responsibility not only become spoiled but actually tend to begin to lose their sense of caring and concern.

During this month reemphasize and redefine the responsibilities you give your children and the dependability you expect of them. Discuss, whenever you get the chance, the responsibilities that others have and how we must be sensitive to the burdens other people have.

*Teach by example and active listening.* Show children the attitude of empathy and the kinds of sensitivity that you want them to mirror. Try to make your own *listening* and *caring* more obvious. One way to do this is "active listening." Instead of the normal parental tendencies of directing, managing, and interrogating children, try to really *hear* what children say. Paraphrase back to them what they have said in a way that reassures them that you heard what they said, have understood it, and are concerned about it. This technique is sometimes also called Rogerian technique after Carl Rogers, the pioneering psychologist who found that people of any age will tell you more if you listen rather than ask.

The practice of active listening will, in addition to encouraging your children to say more to you, set a profound example of the kind of sensitivity you hope they themselves will develop.

––––––

I remember a simple incident that illustrated the effectiveness of this technique:

I sat on the edge of five-year-old Saydi's bed one night and asked her how kindergarten was going. "Fine, Dad," said Saydi, but she didn't look too happy about it. "Well, any problems? Anything you're worried about?"

"Not really, Dad."

It had been a long day for me, and I was really too tired to pry further. I was so tired, I just lay back with Saydi for a minute on her pillow. A minute turned into five minutes—of silence—and I was actually starting to doze off when Saydi said, "Dad, I need a new friend."

It's interesting what kind of responses children's needs tend to trigger in parents' minds. I almost said, "What's wrong? Don't you have enough friends?" Then I almost said, "Was someone mean to you?" "Well, you know, to have friends you have to *be* a friend." Then I almost said, "Hey, *I'm* your friend, you know!"

Those are the typical parental responses. We try to interrogate, or to protect, or to moralize and solve, or to comfort and do a "quick fix."

But this night, maybe because I was so tired, I didn't do any of these things. I just said, "I see, you feel like maybe you could use a new friend."

"Yeah, Dad, because—you know Amy? My old best friend—well, she wasn't so nice to me today."

Again typical responses came to my mind. "What did she do?" or "Were you mean to her?" or "Do I need to call her parents and work this out?"

But again, I just active-listened. "Uh-huh—the *reason* you feel like you need a new friend is that your good friend Amy hasn't been very nice to you."

"Right, Dad, we were playing at recess and she was rude and . . ."

To make a long story short, she went on and on. I laid back there in the dark, hands clasped behind my head, and *listened,* repeating something back to her every few minutes as reinforcement. Saydi told me everything—how she felt, what she liked, what she thought about just about everything. I could never have found out so much by asking. I would not have known the right questions.

—**Richard**

———

*Say "I'm sorry."* Show your children your sensitivity and help them feel sensitive toward you. Whenever you have made a mistake or misjudgment or even been a little insensitive to a child's needs (through your own busy-ness, preoccupation, etc.), go to the child and say you're sorry for not being more in tune and sensitive to what they were worried about or needed.

———

Saydi, now fifteen years old, had come in after her curfew for the third time in a month. I was up late, worrying about her and worrying about not getting any sleep before my early business meeting the next day.

When she finally arrived, I was not just mad, I was *righteously indignant!* Usually feisty Saydi was reduced to tears, and I felt no guilt—she deserved it.

The next day I found out that she had been late because a friend had been hurt and needed help. I went down to her room that evening to apologize (a *very* hard thing for a parent to do!). I got out the first few words, "Saydi, I'm sorry. I didn't know..." But then the old parental instincts took over, "But have you ever heard of telephones? You could have called me. Then I wouldn't have sat up worrying."

Saydi had recovered her feistiness by now and with it her sarcasm. "Oh, yes, Dad," she said, "what is wrong with me? Why didn't I just say to my friend, 'Well, bleed to death. *I* have to go find a phone to call my father'!" The discussion ended worse than the night before!

Finally, the next night, I got off a real apology—and learned something and taught something about sensitivity.   —**Richard**

———

*Make an effort to tell your children how the things they do make you feel.* This will help children be more aware of your feelings and be more sensitive toward them. If a teenager tells you that you are weird, tell him that that hurts your feelings. Sometimes children think of parents as people on whom they can vent their feelings without making a dent. Tell them not only the hurtful things but the positive things. For example, "It makes me feel so happy when I see you cleaning things up without being asked or helping your little brother with his homework."

*Remember that unselfishness does not come naturally.* Try to maintain your patience as you implement this "month." Everyone, although in varying degrees, is born with a certain amount of selfishness. There is no quick fix for learning to be unselfish. It is a process that takes thinking and practicing and a certain amount of maturity to develop.

## Methods for Preschoolers

### "Turns and Timers"

Small children playing together will inevitably want the same toy at the same time. Take the time to sit down with them (over and over) and explain sharing. Help them notice how happy they make the other person when they share with him. Praise even feeble attempts to share.

On occasion use a timer (or an oven clock or alarm clock) that rings when one child's turn is over and it is time to let the other child have his turn.

### Christmas Giving

Give your children some dramatic memories of being unselfish and helping other children with obvious needs. Be a "sub for Santa" and take Christmas to a needy family. Try to link up with a family with children similar in age to your own. Suggest (without pressure) that your child give the corresponding needy child one of his best toys. Point out how little the other child has and how happy a toy would make him.

If possible, observe and take pictures of the receiving child. Follow up with many "recalls" of how happy your child made the other one feel. Praise your child's unselfishness and point out how much joy there is in giving as well as in receiving.

### The "Put Yourself in the Picture" Game

This game lets children practice at empathizing with someone they have never met or spoken to. Watch for pictures in magazines that show people in situations that are unusual to you and your children. These could range from a man on a horse in the mountains to a girl in a magazine clothing ad. Almost any magazine has several pictures or advertisements that will work for this exercise.

The game consists of looking at the picture and attempting to describe how the person in the picture *feels*. This can start on a physical level as you try to imagine what he sees and hears, whether she is cold or warm, and so forth. Then try to go beyond the physical and speculate how he or she might feel emotionally. Have a discussion about it. Let each person imagine how the subject feels and express his or her own observations.

A variation of the game is to give each player a different picture to study, then have them give a short speech or write a brief theme on what the subject feels.

### "How Do You Feel?"

This can help small children be more aware of their own feelings as well as those of others. Use the word *feel* more often. Say, "How do you feel about . . ." or "I feel. . . ." Encourage children to use the word frequently. Discuss feelings whenever the opportunity arises.

### Bedtime Chats

A relaxed atmosphere can be a great help for discussions involving feelings. We've discussed what a good moment bedtime can be for communication, and mentioned various fun questions to ask children at bedtime. Try during this month to expand this idea a little so that it includes the expression of more specific feelings.

Start it off yourself by sitting on the edge of a child's bed and volunteering how you have felt about various things during the day. Let the child respond in kind. Prompt him or her along with questions, encouragement, and compliments.

Don't expect feelings to flow as freely as you may wish on the first few efforts. Be content to talk about your feelings a few times and be patient about your child's expressions.

---

The only problem with "bedroom chats" is that we parents are sometimes more tired than our children.

The other night I sat on the edge of our son's bed, told him a short story, and then asked how he was feeling.

I decided to lie down by him while he told me about some things at school that day.

The next thing I knew, it was morning and my son was waking me up.

"You slept here all night, Dad. You were so funny. I was telling you about school and you kept saying, 'Uh-huh,' and then you just starting snoring. I went up and told Mom and she said, 'Just let Dad sleep. He needs it!' " —**Richard**

### The "How Does He Feel?" Game

Tell your children the following scenarios and ask the question at the end.

- Janie was in the car with all her friends on the way to preschool. Emily started talking about her birthday party on Saturday. Julie said she loved clowns and couldn't wait to see the magic tricks. Jodie said she liked the cute invitation Emily had brought. Janie realized that she was the only one in the car who had not received an invitation to Emily's party. How do you think she felt?

- After playing with trucks all afternoon together, David decided that he wanted to play house. He wanted to be the daddy and he wanted Jeremy to be the little boy. "I don't want to be the little boy," yelled Jeremy, "I want to be the daddy!" "Well, I don't want to play with you anymore then and I'm going home," announced David. How do you think Jeremy felt?

Talk about possible solutions for the above dilemmas.

## Methods for Elementary School Age

### The "Big E" Award

As with all award methods, give recurrent, notice-able, lasting praise. At Sunday dinner (or whatever time you have specified for awards), say, "Who's in the run-ning for the 'Big E' award?" *E* stands for empathy, and each family member should think through the week just passed and try to come up with incidents when he no-ticed how someone else felt and sympathized enough to say or do something to help someone or at least ac-knowledge what he noticed.

### Memorizing

This is an effective way to plant, clearly and last-ingly, the concept of unselfishness and sensitivity in older elementary-age children's minds. Together mem-orize G. K. Chesterton's statement: "Love of one's neighbor is the only door out of the dungeon of self."

Discuss it with children. Ask what it means. Point out and discuss why selfishness and self-centeredness is a dungeon.

For older children consider memorizing Emerson's quote "See how the masses of men worry themselves into nameless graves while here and there, a great un-selfish soul *forgets himself* into immortality."

### The Noticing Game

This game trains children to see more that is outside themselves and thus to be less self-aware. Form a habit of playing "the noticing game" when you are traveling or going to any unfamiliar place with children. Ask them, without notice or warning, to close and cover their eyes. Then ask them to describe, as best they can, the room or scene they are in (the walls, the lighting, the carpet, the trees, the sky, etc.). Let them also play the game on you. The exercise in observing and being aware of where you are and what is around you is good training for empathy and sensitivity.

### The Nose-Watching Game

This game will further increase children's awareness of other people. While on a trip or outing together—or even while shopping or running errands—see how many different kinds of noses you can observe. Later discuss the most interesting noses you noticed and how no two are alike.

### The Looking-and-Listening-for-Needs Game

This can help children begin focusing the seeing and listening skills on opportunities for service. Tell the children that this game is an extension of the nose-watching game. Only this time we'll be looking not at people's noses but at their needs. Explain that needs are a lot harder to see than noses. To see needs, you have to look hard and listen hard. Someone might be feeling just a little discouraged and need some encouragement, or a little insecure and need a compliment. Or someone might feel left out and need a friend, or useless and need to be asked to help. Or there might be more obvious needs like a hungry child or a lonely older person.

Select a day for the game, a day when you can be together for dinner in the evening. During the day keep track of how many needs you can notice and identify. Take notes. At dinner that night give reports on those notes and discuss and compare them.

### The Secret-Buddies Game

This game helps children shift their attention to another family member and experience the satisfaction of doing things for that person anonymously. Put each family member's name (including parents') in a hat and let each person draw a name secretly. Spend a week playing "secret buddies," during which each person tries to find little things he or she can do for his buddy anonymously (from carefully anonymous notes, compliments, and gifts, to fixing or cleaning secretly). At the end of the week give a prize for "best deeds" and another for "best secrecy."

### The "Whose Problem?" Verbal Exercise

This will help children react less to the cruelty of other children and be more careful of being cruel themselves. Whenever an example or instance of teasing or meanness or peer abuse comes to your attention, take the opportunity to explain that children who behave in such ways almost *always* do so because they are mistreated by someone else or because they feel insecure. Get in the habit of asking, "Why do you think he did that?" or "Whose problem is that?" Explore possibilities. (Maybe his parents are unkind to him. Maybe his big brother picks on him. Maybe he's not doing well in school and needs to prove himself by showing he's bigger or stronger.) Discuss the possibilities in a sensitive, empathetic way.

### "Create Your Own"

This activity will help children express their own unique feelings and enhance their creativity. Instead of buying birthday cards, "get well soon" cards, Mother's Day cards, and so on, encourage children to make their own, writing prose or poetry to sensitively express how they feel about another person. *Praise* their every attempt.

### The Adjective Game

This game assists children in defining their feelings and increases their ability to verbalize those feelings. As a family make a long list of adjectives that describe how people can feel. Start with the most basic feelings, such as "happy," "sad," "mad," "frustrated," "embarrassed," and move to more specific and interesting adjectives, such as "murky," "jumpy," "agitated," "perplexed," "elated."

Try to list at least one hundred words before you are finished. Explain that a good vocabulary helps us figure out our feelings as well as express them.

Hang the list in a visible place and invite family members to add to it whenever they think of another good descriptive adjective or whenever they feel an emotion that is not described by any word on the list.

## Methods for Adolescents

### Journals and Poetry

Help your children express and thus explore and enhance their sensitivity. Be sure a child has a journal or diary. Keep one yourself. Encourage the expression of feelings. Teach children to begin many sentences in their journal with the words *I feel* . . . . Make poetry a common practice, even a tradition in your family. If *you* write poetry, and if you encourage and praise every attempt of your children, they will learn to enjoy it. And poetry is a great *teacher* as well as expresser of sensitive feelings.

———

We have a tradition of writing poems to Linda on her birthday. The poems are always more treasured than any other gift. Some examples (excerpts) from one "birthday book":

Seventeen-year-old Saren wrote:

### You Were There

*I remember*
*Watching the cracks in the ceiling move,*
*Laying on the waterbed,*
*So sick with some forgotten malady.*
*And I was so small.*
*But you were there.*
*I fell off my bike,*
*Raked my skin on the cruel gravel.*
*But you were there.*
*I felt discouraged,*
*Dejected, alone—But still,*
*You were there.*
*I came home late and got up late*
*I argued with everything you said*
*I missed the bus,*
*I hardly said thanks*

*But always and forever,*
*You were there.*

**Sixteen-year-old Shawni wrote:**

MOTHER'S TOUCH

*The child murmurs softly,*
*Crying quietly of his troubles*
*The day has been cold and bitter*
*And the echos of the painful scoffs and cruel laughter*
*Run endlessly through his head*
*And they feel to him like pounding thunder.*

*The tender touch of mother*
*The peaceful, pleasant feelings.*
*And the sweet soothing voice,*
*"Hush," she whispers,*
*And her voice sounds like velvet.*
*The child's contented figure stirs quietly,*
*Wrapped in the warmth of his mother's touch.*

**14 year-old Josh wrote:**

*Who is a person so kind and loving,*
*And always willing to help?*

*Who is a person that can raise nine children,*
*Keep the house clean,*
*And rarely lose her temper?*

*Well, this person is my mom,*
*And I love her so.*
*She's so peaceful and nice, yes,*
*This person's my mom.*

Twelve-year-old Saydi wrote:

## MY MOTHER'S SWEET SMILE

*My mother can tell me so much in her face,*
*Her cheerful smiling mouth can tell me the case.*
*She shows me she's happy, worried, or sad,*
*Angry, excited, or extremely glad.*
*She shows me I'm special, that there's no one like*
*me*
*That I can be someone and that I am free.*
*I watch her smile stand in crowded places*
*And I'm glad she's my mom, seeing all the dull faces*
*With her sweet sensitive smile, she says "I love you"*
*I proudly smile back, for I love her too.*

Ten-year-old Jonah (who was aware that Linda had a head cold) wrote:

> *You are like a big blue sky and a bright sun to lite*
> *up many lives or help us.*
> *And you are like a teacher at home and not at school.*
> *You make my life much easier.*
> *And you are very beautiful.*
> *I love you, I hope you're feeling better.*
>
> *Love from,*
> *Jonah*

And, just to illustrate that it's not only adolescents who can write poetry, eight-year-old Talmadge wrote:

> *You are like a butuful spontaineaus*
> *horse that alwas has to work*
> *for her babies.*

*You are sophisticated and
sensative.
You have the sweetest smile.*

> *Love,
> Talmadge*

*P.S. I love you*

And seven-year-old Noah wrote:

*Mom, you are
Sweet as candy
Pretty as a flower
Soft as a cushion
Nice as Santa
And pritty as a girlfriend.*

*Happy Birthday, Mom!*

## The Mirror-Window Lesson

This can help adolescents conceptualize and appreciate the difference between self-centeredness and extra-centeredness. Try to get a piece of one-way glass (mirror from one side, window from other). If you can't find one, a plain piece of glass will do. Point out that when it is dark behind the glass, it is a mirror—all you see in it is yourself. When it is *light* behind it, you see *through* it—you see other people and not your own reflection. Point out to your children that life is much the same. When our minds are dark and self-centered, we only see ourselves ("What's best for me?" "How will that affect me?" "What can this person do for me?") In this mode we are always unhappy and self-conscious. But when we *light* up and look at other people—trying to listen, trying to see their needs, and so on—we "lose ourselves" and quit worrying about ourselves and feeling self-conscious.

### Three Daily Priorities—the Three S's

This can help adolescents become effective goal setters and ensure that they think of extra-centered as well as self-centered possibilities or goals. Help children get into the habit of spending five minutes each morning setting up three simple goals for the day ahead.

**1.** The most important thing they can do that day for *school* (a particularly important test, assignment, etc.)

**2.** The single most important thing they can do for *themselves* that day (eat well, exercise, get enough rest, etc.)

**3.** One key thing that they can do for *someone else* that day (help a little brother or sister with something, be nice to an unpopular person at school, pay a particular person a compliment, etc.).

The idea is to get children to stop to think about three priorities for a few moments each day (school, self, and service). Just asking the three questions will help an adolescent get his mind above his own worries and insecurities. And doing one important thing each day in each area will give you, the parent, a great many opportunities for praise and encouragement!

### The Listen-Paraphrase-and-Add-Feeling Game

This game will help improve children's listening and interpretation skills. Explain to children that the listening ability your family worked on earlier is just the start for being able to understand other people's feelings. You have to listen, understand, and then try hard to put yourself into the other person's shoes and imagine what he feels.

Then introduce the following listening game: One family member asks another what happened to him that day. The second person tells some experience, and the first person repeats back or paraphrases the experience, visualizing it as though it had happened to him. He then indicates how he thinks the other person felt.

For example, twelve-year-old James says to ten-year-old Pat, "What happened today?" Pat says, "Oh, we had a math test and I thought it would be easy, but the teacher asked a lot of questions from the chapter I didn't study and hardly any from the chapter I did!"

James responds, "So you thought you were prepared for the test, because you did study, but you mostly studied one chapter, and when you took the test, most of it was on another chapter—one that you hadn't studied. I'll bet you felt kind of frustrated, and maybe you felt a little bit mad at your teacher for tricking you or for not telling you what chapter to study."

It's surprising how much children enjoy this kind of discussion (once they get the hang of it) with their siblings or with their parents.

And there is no better training for the development of real concern.

### Miss a Meal for a Purpose

This can help children empathize physically and become more acquainted with the basic idea of trying to feel others' needs. From age eight, and often earlier, children are capable of fasting for at least one meal. With the kind of discussion and observations that parents can add, this can be one of the most basic and meaningful early empathetic experiences they have. Talk about the feeling of hunger as it is experienced and about how it might feel if it went on for days if they, like nearly one-third of the children in the world, went to bed hungry each night.

This method is particularly instructive if you can use the money you save by missing a meal to help someone who is hungry. Some families sponsor a child in a Third World country through one of the relief organizations; they receive pictures and letters from a real human being who is being fed by the money they save through fasting.

As children come to understand and appreciate the idea of missing a meal to help someone else, they will feel a physical empathy, which can be a good start toward feeling the deeper forms of emotional, social, and even spiritual empathy. As you talk about how hunger feels, ask also how they think people feel who have no friends or whose parents do not care about them.

### Sponsoring a Child in an Underdeveloped Country

This gives children the chance to serve others who are both very different and very far away from themselves. Another way to make service essentially anonymous is to give it to people who are too far away or too far removed from you to "pay you back" in any way. Various organizations offer opportunities (for a few dollars per month) to sponsor a child—paying for physical support and often for education.

You can make your support strictly anonymous, receiving information only from the organization and not corresponding directly with the child. But there is so much enjoyment and so much benefit in having your children correspond directly with the child that you may want to settle for "semi-anonymous" service in this case.

# Kindness and Friendliness

*Awareness that being kind and considerate is more admirable than being tough or strong. The tendency to understand rather than confront. Gentleness, particularly toward those who are younger or weaker. The ability to make and keep friends. Helpfulness. Cheerfulness.*

———

Our oldest daughter had turned seventeen, was a high school senior, and was looking at universities and trying to decide where to apply. One day we visited a women's college and had a particularly pleasant and agreeable experience. As we left, we were discussing our feelings and trying to sort out just what it was that made this school and this campus so appealing and left us with such a good taste and such a good feeling.

The campus was beautiful, the course offerings were varied and interesting, but there was no particular thing about either that we could put our finger on as the cause of the warm feeling we had.

Then we realized that it was the consistent and sincere courtesy and friendliness of the people we had met. There seemed to be a tradition there not only of politeness but of going beyond the expected and being truly friendly and kind. Everyone extended a greeting. Everyone went out of their way to smile and make eye contact.

It was the expected manner of behavior at the school and it impressed (and warmed) us more than any of the academic reputations or the physical facilities.

—**Richard**

---

Simple kindness and friendliness is a great human value. It involves parts of other values, such as the empathy of *sensitivity* and the boldness of *courage,* but it is a very separate and different value from these. This value is also partially an extension of the value of peaceability. In peaceability we try to teach children not to hurt and to avoid conflicts. Here we teach the positive side of *being* a friend, *acting* friendly and kind, and becoming more polite and courteous.

Friendliness and gentleness also apply to *self.* Children who learn to be gentle and tolerant with themselves grow up to be less stressed and more relaxed and self-secure.

Simple friendliness (based on our earlier-established criteria and definition of a value of something that *helps* others and diminishes *hurt* in others) is a profound value. Often a simple act of kindness or a word or two of extended friendship can change another person's attitude and mood for the rest of a day—and longer.

In trying to teach kindness and friendliness to our children we once again realize that they are not lumps of clay to be molded as we choose, but seedlings—already who they are—ready to blossom if watered and fertilized and exposed to a lot of sunlight.

———

It might be interesting to note that even though we have managed to blossom a little, Richard and I were both very shy children. Two-thirds of our children also have shy tendencies in varying degrees and none has escaped the uncomfortable feeling of wondering if their friends will be nice to them that day. I remember as a young adolescent being so painfully shy that it was hard even to look at another person, let alone talk to someone.

Some of my childhood memories are very clear because they were so painful. And some of the feelings and the worry about not having friends are easy to recall. I've found that telling these experiences to our children and explaining that they are natural and normal for many children is the most productive and helpful thing I can do. Children who realize that their shyness is normal cease to worry about it as much, and as they decrease worrying, they also lose some of their shyness. **—Linda**

———

Wherever your children fit on the scale of natural kindness and friendliness to others, there is always room for improvement on this important value of life.

———

A friend of mine told me a story that I thought illustrated how parents can be kind and friendly to their own children and thus improve the rapport and feeling between them.

He came home from work one day, went into his "private" bathroom, and found little five-year-old Lulu, who loved trying to clean things, holding an empty cleanser can and standing over a bathtub that was overflowing with soap suds onto the carpet. He nearly reacted the way most parents would have: "Lulu! You used way too much soap! You're ruining the carpet! You should never try to do things like this without help!"

But he had some especially tender feelings in his heart that day for Lulu, and he said, "Oh, Lu, you were trying to clean Dad's tub, weren't you?"

Little Lulu looked down and said, "But Daddy, I used way too much soap!" It was a tender, warm moment that ended in a big hug.

If the father had said, "You used way too much soap," Lulu would have said, probably with some bitterness or some hurt, "But Daddy, I was just trying to clean your tub!" It would have been an unpleasant, separating moment.

—**Richard**

Sometimes we don't need to tell our children what they did wrong. They already know. If we are kind and gentle with them and come to their defense, *they* will say what we would have said, and the moment will be warm and the feeling will be right.

## GENERAL GUIDELINES

*Teach by example.* Give your children clear and specific models for friendliness, kindness, and politeness. This value is one that cannot be overdone. During the month be *extra* friendly and polite to everyone, including your children. Use "please," "thank you," and "excuse me," profusely. Say nice things. Practice Emily Post etiquette in everything from opening doors and holding chairs for women to setting the table in a proper and special way. Even help children with their own jobs. Smile a lot.

Watch children respond. Once they get over the suspicion that you're putting them on or rehearsing for a part in some play, they will begin to mirror what they see in you.

*Have a "gentleness and politeness pact."* This can create a mood of particular kindness and warmth in your home during this "month." Get together as a family as you start this month and discuss how pleasant a place the world is when people are kind and gentle. Ask the children to join you in a "pact of gentleness and politeness" for the month. Explain that this will mean a commitment of two "do's" and two "don't's."

Do's: • Be polite—say, "please," "thank you," and "excuse me," and look for chances to extend acts of courtesy.

• Smile and ask, "How are you?" Expect a real answer to the question and *listen* to it.

Don't's: • Don't yell or raise your voice or be critical of another.

• Don't say anything critical—neither of someone else nor of yourself. (No "I'm so stupid" or "I can't do anything right.")

Talk frequently about how things are going, how people feel, how hard it is to remember, and so on.

*Decide where your child stands in his natural abilities to be kind and friendly.* Know what your challenge is with each child. There is nothing quite like the joy one feels as a result of kindnesses to those who really need and appreciate it, whether it be a good deed for one little old man across the street or kindness on a more grander scale. However, kindness and friendliness are never as easy as they sound. Some children show their insecurities by pretending to be popular but putting other children down in ways that are outright cruel, while other shrinking violets and painfully shy children spend all their time wondering why no one likes them. Others are genuinely well adjusted and naturally look for ways to be kind and friendly to those around them. Try to determine where your child fits in his natural abilities to be kind and friendly so that you know where to begin.

*Encourage children of all ages to look people straight in the eye when they speak to them.* This method, used earlier in the courage chapter, can also help children to convey interest and friendliness. For two of our shyest children, eye contact with adults seems almost impossible. One particularly must have decided before she was born not to speak to adults (other than family and close friends) unless it was an absolute emergency. For children like these, practice sessions before leaving for an encounter with an adult or a new child in the neighborhood would be very helpful. You play the role of the adult if they are going to speak to an adult (a new teacher, for example) and have them practice looking straight in your eye and say something like, "It's very nice to meet you." The dialogue will depend on the situation. Use another child in the family or a friend for the "rehearsal" if you need to polish up a bit before going to meet a new child in the neighborhood.

*Encourage your child's friends to come to your house.* Although you may have to force yourself to tolerate the extra mess and noise, it is very valuable for you to see your children interacting with their friends. Actively listen to their conversation if you can do it without making it seem like eavesdropping.

We have been amazed at some of the interactions our children have had with friends. It gives us real insight into their patterns of thinking and helps us to help them be better friends through a little more thoughtfulness. We're even glad to know about the startlingly honest outbursts from preschoolers, such as "Go home. I don't want to play with you anymore!"

*Teach your child the value of relationships, not only with friends but with family.* This will increase their appreciation of close "blood" relationships. During an evening meal every few months take the time to reinforce the importance of having friends and being a friend. Foster and nourish the idea that even though outside friends are very important, the best friends they will ever have should be their brother or sister (as well as his or her parents). Childhood friends will come and go, but family members will last throughout life. Those friendships should be nurtured and treated with care. You could even try a private game among family members. When one child is persecuting another or arguing or calling names in a way that he would not think of doing with a friend, have the persecuted child say the word *friend,* which is a code word to the other child to lay off and begin treating him a little more like a friend. Although it may not work at the moment, it will help to raise the awareness of what they're doing. (The same game works for parents who talk to their children in less than glowing terms, or vice versa.) You could even suggest that when a child is angry or being rude to another family member, an onlooking child has a responsibility to walk up to the child being attacked, put his arm around him, and say, "Don't talk that way to one of my best friends."

*The Comp Award.* Encourage your children to find something they like about their friends and compliment them on it. At Sunday dinner we give a Comp Award to the child who can recall and tell about the nicest compliment given to another person. Use the giving of the award to generate a discussion about how to notice things and give sincere and specific compliments. Talk about what a compliment can do for its recipient.

## Methods for Preschoolers

### The "Magic" Words

*Intrigue* small children with the notion of using polite words. Tell the children any story that involves magic words—*abracadabra, Rumpelstiltskin*—or any story you want to make up. Then ask them if there is such a thing as *real* magic words—words that make good things happen when they are used.

The answer is yes. "Please," "thank you," "excuse me," and "you're welcome" make people smile, make them feel better, make the world work better.

Explain this notion several times and prepare your children for the simple correction or reminder, "Remember to use the magic words."

### The Ugly-Fish Game

This game is a good way to help small children begin to grasp the idea that kindness can actually change the *nature* of those it is practiced upon. Put children on a coffee table, or chair, or couch and have them imagine that whatever they are on is a boat and that you are an "ugly fish" swimming around in the water (on the floor). Snap at them and growl and say, "I'm an ugly fish and I'm mean and I don't like anybody!" Encourage the kids to say something like, "You're not ugly. You're rather nice looking." Then instantly "transform" before their very eyes—smile, calm down, and say, "I am? Oh . . . well. I'm sorry I snapped at you."

Then let the children say you're ugly, and transform back. When they treat you nicely, turn nice again. Tell the preschoolers that people are like ugly fish. If you treat them nice, they become nice. If you treat them mean, they become mean.

### Thumper's Motto

Give small children a particular motto of friendliness that they can memorize and that you can use on them as a reminder and a guide. If possible, go see Walt Disney's *Bambi* (or, better yet, rent the video and watch it at home). Watch for (and replay, if it's a video) Thumper's little speech on "If you can't say sumpthin' nice, don't say anythin' at all."

Have small children memorize that line. Explain to them that there really is no place for bad or unkind words—silence is better. But it is best to think of something nice to say.

When there is a problem, ask, "What is Thumper's motto?" Let the child repeat it to you and tell him you expect him to follow it.

### Story: "The Real Hero"

Telling this story will help small children consider the fact that being friendly and kind is better than being tough and strong. Paraphrase the basic story and expand on it in your own words:

Once there were two friends who lived in a place called Anywhere. As they grew up, they became very different from each other. One of them became huge and strong and developed super-powers. He became known as Muscle Man. The other became very friendly and kind but had no superpowers at all. He became known as Polite Man.

One year a group of aliens arrived in a space-ship from a far-distant galaxy. The aliens landed and asked to be taken to the leader of Anywhere. They were taken to Muscle Man. Muscle Man, when he saw them, assumed that they were bad aliens. He immediately tried to fight them using his strength to try to tie them up. But their pow-ers were greater than Muscle Man's, and they tied him up. Then they said, "This can't be your true leader. Take us to him."

This time they were taken to Polite Man. He welcomed the aliens in a friendly way and asked if he could do anything for them. They thanked him and said they had been sent as the "friendly force" of the universe and told to bring all un-friendly or warlike people to the universe court to be locked up, but that they were simply to give greetings and best wishes to those who were already friendly and polite. They said they were pleased that the town of Anywhere was led by a person like Polite Man.

### Have the Child Choose Someone for Whom He'd Like to Do a Good Deed

This teaches small children the feelings of joy that comes from giving. The person could range from a best friend to a kind, elderly neighbor. Then take a plate of cookies or a flower to them. Kindnesses performed together can be some of life's most memorable experiences.

### The Kindness Game

One way to teach little children the definition of kindness is by playing a game with them. Use the following as a test scenario. Then fill in with your own examples:

Say, "I'm going to tell you about some little children and you tell me whether what they do is kind or unkind."

- Timmy is invited to play at Rob's house, but after he's been there about a half hour, he says, "I'm tired of playing with you. I'm going to Zachary's house." Kind or unkind? Why?
- Sarah is playing with Jane when she suddenly says, "You have really pretty red hair!" Kind or unkind? Why?
- And so on—make up your own.

## Methods for Elementary School Age

### The Icebreaker Award

Encourage your children to initiate conversation and make new friends. Have a card with an I.B. on it. Use the usual Sunday procedure for awards, asking who's in the running for the Icebreaker Award. Encourage children to think through the week past and recall any instance when they introduced themselves, started a conversation, made a new friend, and so on. Give praise and encouragement for every effort.

### Define *Gentleman*

Help your children—particularly boys—adopt the conscious goal of politeness. Ask children why invitations and speeches are often addressed to "ladies and gentlemen"? Ask, "What is a gentleman and what is a lady?" Point out that politeness has always been a mark of respect and desirability. Ask, "What is the point of the word *gentle* being part of *gentlemen?* Are men supposed to be gentle? Is it manly and macho to be gentle and polite?" Point out that all great people *are* gentle and polite, because they wish to help rather than to hurt.

Tell stories that emphasize how gentleness often goes hand in hand with strength—for example the Bible story of Samson; *The Gentle Giant* (a children's book), and so on.

### The "Catch an Eye" Contest

This gives children practice in the friendly art of direct eye contact. When you are going somewhere with one or more children, particularly to a public place, have a contest to see who can "catch the most eyes." To count someone, you must look at them until they glance back, then smile as you catch their eye. Count the ones that smile back and count separately the ones that don't. The "smile-backers" are worth two points, the "glance but don't smile" people are worth one point.

———

I was at a shopping mall with three of our children (ages nine, eleven, and twelve) one day when we held our first "catch an eye" contest. The game got quite competitive, and each of the children ended up with a score of over one hundred.

Afterward, as we were driving home, Saydi observed, "It's amazing how many people just look away the minute you catch their eye."

Jonah added, "Yes, and they're not near as fun as the ones who look back at you and smile. I think those are the happy ones." —**Richard**

———

### Memorize

Remind children, on an ongoing basis, of this value. Learn the phrase, "A man convinced against his will is of the same opinion still." Explain to older elementary-age children the difference between win-lose and win-win. Explain that winning in a discussion or personal conflict that causes another person to lose may not be good at all. (You can "win the battle but lose the war.") When people are friendly and kind, a solution can usually be found that makes both people happy.

### The "Friend" Chart and Contest

This will help children concentrate on friendliness and new acquaintances during this "month." Put up a blank chart in the kitchen with each family member's name at the top of a separate vertical column. Have a contest to see who can meet the most new people during the month, writing the names in their column. The requirement is to learn to know the name plus one essential fact about a person they had not met before.

You can join the contest with the child or children and spruce up your own friend-making and conversational skills.

### The Chain-Letter Comparison

Help children grasp the "chain reaction" nature of friendliness and kindness. If your child has participated in a chain letter, point out that one letter leads to so many more. Explain that friendliness is similar. When we are kind to a person, it is much more likely that that person will be kind to someone else. A similar comparison can be made (or a demonstration) with dominoes set up to create a chain reaction.

### Teach Your Children How to Deal with Cruelty

You can protect them against other children's cruelty and sensitize them to trying to avoid the characteristic in themselves. Although teasing, unkindness—downright cruelty—is apparent at every age, we have found it is particularly prevalent in elementary-age children. Unkindness can be handled much better if you teach your children two concepts. First, children who are really cruel almost universally do it as an outgrowth of their own insecurities. Almost inevitably they are experiencing problems at home or some kind of identity crisis. Cruelty is really that child's problem. If the victim of the child's mistreatment takes the abuse too seriously, then it becomes his problem too.

Second, something can usually be done about the problem of cruelty. If the child can tell his parents about the problem, the very telling will help. Although it is difficult for a sixth-grader to tell his tormentor how his unkindness makes him feel, it sometimes helps. For difficult or extreme cases, parent and child may need to meet the other parent and child. Although it's sometimes embarrassing for parents and kids alike, this kind of meeting can work wonders.

---

When Joshua was ten, he went through a period when he was being teased mercilessly by some of the boys in his class. A lot of the teasing stemmed from Josh's disinterest in sports. Twin boys were the ring leaders, and Josh began coming home from school every day saying that he didn't want to go tomorrow.

We tried to help him think of things to say to the boys, then we tried to encourage him to ignore them. Nothing helped. They knew they were getting to Josh, and matters just got worse. The twins were not only teasing but shoving Josh, calling him a chicken, and asking him why he didn't dare fight them.

I finally decided it was time to go see these twins and their parents at their home. Josh *hated* the idea. He begged me not to go, and when I told him I was going and wanted him to come with me, he really panicked. "No, Dad, no, I promise I won't mention it again. I'll work it out myself, don't worry."

But by then I was convinced we should go. I finally calmed Josh down, and we drove to the address we found in the school directory.

As so often happens, so much was explained by the parents and the home. The father was on his way to a karate club. He was a military, macho kind of a guy, and his boys were imitating him. But he was responsive to my concerns. He had his boys apologize to Josh, and then the three of them spent a little time together while the dad and I talked.

Afterward (for days afterward) I praised Josh for the courage he'd shown in going over there with me, and we talked together about why those boys acted the way they did. —**Richard**

---

Although we hate to admit it, sometimes *our* child is the one making another child miserable. In such cases we may realize that the problem is not that we have taught our child to be mean to another. The problem is that we haven't taught him enough about being kind and sensitive to others. Maybe we also have not taught him well enough that the feelings of others are fragile and crucial to their overall well-being. In these cases we can console ourselves by realizing that it is never too late.

---

One week I discovered that our fifth-grader was not being very kind to a friend who had been spending lots of time at our house because his parents worked and were not home until late evening. "I'm not going to play with Jared so much anymore because when people see me with him, they think I must not be too popular if I spend a lot of time with him," he stated in his very matter-of-fact fifth-grade way. A long discussion followed about kindness and friendliness. When it was over, I think both of us felt a little wiser (and maybe a little more mature! —**Linda**

---

### Teach Children to Look for Those Who Have Been Left Out

This will help open their perspective and see opportunities for friendliness and love. Although sometimes it takes a little more maturity than elementary school children possess, it is important to raise their awareness of the children who are being left out and to encourage them to try extra hard to *include* these children. One evening we asked our boys to name a few children who were being left out or teased by their peers. They easily thought of several. We asked them to do something about it the next day and report back at dinnertime. The stories were not only heartwarming, they were ongoing. Some of those left-out children became good friends.

## Methods for Adolescents

### Have a Dinner Party

This can help children focus on manners, politeness, and general friendliness. While it is a lot of trouble, a dinner party is a wonderful way to get children exposed to a pleasant situation of manners and conversation. Invite people who will foster friendliness. "Dress-rehearse" (with children) table manners, introduction methods, eye contact during conversation, what questions to ask, and so on.

### Name Remembering

It's a good idea to help adolescents learn to remember the names of people they meet. Discuss with children the importance of people's names. (The most important word to anyone is his own name!) Point out that remembering names is a great key in the art of making friends. Teach children that there are two techniques that work best to remember a name. One is to use the name several times in the conversation you have when you meet a person. Say, "Nice to meet you, *Joyce*. Where do you live, *Joyce*? *Joyce,* do you have a brother who works at Miller's?" Another is to write the name down (on your planner, appointment book, notebook, etc.) as soon as possible after you meet. At the end of the day glance at the name again, associate it with the face, and it will be yours forever (or at least for some time).

### Smile, Ask, Listen

Help your children remember the three "keys to friendliness." Ask them to remember the three words they all had to learn when they were small in order to cross streets safely ("stop, look, and listen"). Tell them that there is another simple three-word phrase that will help them to be automatically friendly and well liked. The phrase is "smile, ask, and listen." Talk about each word . . . how a smile brightens the day for those who give and receive the smile. How a question gets conversations started and lets the other person know you are interested in him. And how really listening helps you learn about and know someone—and shows him that you care.

Make "Smile, ask, and listen" your family motto for this "month." Exemplify it to your children and talk with them about it at every opportunity.

### Learning from History

A brief discussion will help adolescents appreciate politeness and manners. At a dinner table or while driving or some other moment you are with your children, ask questions like: "Why do we do things the way we do? (Make cars or airplanes? Have traffic laws and speed limits? Make food according to recipes? Etc.)" Steer the conversation so that the answer to all these questions is "because it *works*." After you have established the idea of learning from what has worked in the past rather than rediscovering everything by trial and error, ask the key question: "Why should we practice politeness and manners?" Make sure children understand that the answer is the same: "That they *work*." People and societies have discovered the behavior that is best for everyone. These codes are called politeness and manners.

### Teach Them That Maturity Begins When They Can "See Through Windows Instead of into Mirrors"

This will help adolescents conceptualize the problem of selfishness and the solution of empathy.

------

I admired a certain girl in high school very much. She was a year older than I, so that made her (in my mind at least) too old to be really close friends with. But I watched her and decided I wanted to be more like her. Instead of her being worried about which boys liked her or what others would think of her, like so many of the kids her age, I noticed that she was always nice to everyone, especially the mentally challenged girl whom others either made fun of or tried to ignore. Whenever I talked to her, she complimented me and asked me about my life. I could never get her to talk about herself very long. She always seemed sincerely interested in everyone else and was always careful to include everyone in a conversation—even a stupid little "underclassman" like me. Even though she wasn't the most beautiful or stylish girl in the school, everyone loved her. She easily won the election for student-body secretary and "Most Likely to Succeed," even though she often campaigned for her opponents.   **—Linda**

------

We've told this story to our children often—to the point that they must feel like they know her. The point is that life becomes much more secure and mature when we can look through the windows of our lives and see the needs of others instead of allowing everything to reflect back on us as does a mirror.

### Remind Adolescents That in Order to Have a Friend, One Must Be a Friend.

This will increase their daily awareness of friends and their needs. Thoughtful kindnesses such as taking ice cream to a friend who has just had her wisdom teeth out or dropping off a little flower just before a big event in a friend's life, are moments that will never be forgotten.

### Teach Them That You Can Learn Something from Everyone, Even If They're "Weird"

This can help "open up" children's attitudes to other people who are very dissimilar to them. Often teenagers feel they can only be friends with people who are like they are. What a great slice of life they miss!

---

After a P.E. class one day Kristen, a friend's daughter at the junior high, began to talk to a girl who identified herself as a "rocker" by wearing black clothes and a wild hairdo sprayed orange and green. She found the girl to be a good conversationalist and continued the relationship. After a week Kristen's friends confronted her. "Why do you spend your time with her?' they asked. "You're a cheerleader and you have your reputation to think about! What do you see in her? We're scared of her. You'd better watch out!"

Kristen filled the unthinking girls in on what she had learned about her new

222

friend the rocker during the past week. When she was eleven, she had seen her uncle shoot and kill her father. Her mother was an alcoholic, and she went home each day to an empty, topsy-turvy house. Kristen had wisely figured out that her manner of dress was her cry for attention. As a result Kristen's friends gained new respect for her, and new tolerance for the other girl.   —**Linda**

———————

# Justice
# and Mercy

*Obedience to law, fairness in work and play. An understanding of natural consequences and the law of the harvest. A grasp of mercy and forgiveness and an understanding of the futility (and bitter poison) of carrying a grudge.*

*Justice* and *mercy*—these words seem too abstract, multifaceted, maybe even too religious for children to understand. Yet when they are broken down into their simplest form, they are the basic values for every household—the values around which everything else revolves.

---

On one of our media tours to publicize our books, we found ourselves on a nationally syndicated TV talk show with a live audience. Although we had done many such shows, this audience somehow seemed different. As we got into the show, we realized what the difference was. The host asked us what we thought was the best place to start in raising a family. We quickly answered that probably most important was establishing family laws—just a few—from the time children were small, so that they would know their parameters, know what was expected, and have a sense of justice and fairness.

To our amazement the audience disagreed. One mother raised her hand and said she'd never think of punishing her son, because he was bigger than she now and he'd probably hit her back. The hour we spent with these people was very interesting. Many of them personified the products of a home without laws, justice, or mercy.   **—Linda**

---

There is both security and unity in the justice and fairness that exists in a home. The beginning lies in the developing of clear family laws and providing for repentance and apology as well as for consistent justice.

---

Perhaps the two most important things we've ever learned in our family about justice and mercy were taught to us by our oldest daughter as she was growing up. The first lesson came when she was about seven. We had tried to set up some "family laws" for her and her five-year-old sister. We had done so democratically by asking them to suggest laws. We wrote their suggestions on a list, along with our own and ended up with twenty-four family laws, ranging from "don't hit anyone" to "don't plug in plugs."

One Sunday seven-year-old Saren came home from Sunday school with a suggestion. "Dad and Mom," she said, "I think we've got way too many laws. I can't even remember half of them. I learned today that Heavenly Father only gave us ten laws! We need to simplify!"

And simplify we did. We worked our list down to five one-word laws that each child knew and understood, we connected them with natural-consequence punishments, and we felt that we at least were beginning to teach the value of justice in our family. (Suggested family laws and punishments appear on pages 227 through 229.)

About three years later this same oldest daughter, now ten, reminded us of the other principle that needs to go hand in hand with justice. Again it was Sunday, and again we had just returned from Sunday school. One of her little brothers had become angry with his sister and pushed her down. We were in the process of administering the punishment of sending the boy to his room, but Saren noticed the look on his face, which said he was sorry for what he'd done and concerned that he had hurt his sister. "You know, Dad," Saren said, "if someone is sorry and wants to apologize and promise not to do it again, he shouldn't have to have the punishment. In the Bible they call it repenting." **—Richard**

Saren was right of course. One reason for repentance is to avoid punishment. And more is often learned from repenting than from being punished. Our five family laws now carry provisions for repentance and thus give us frequent opportunities to learn the two most difficult (and perhaps most important) skills of life—namely to *repent* or improve and to *forgive*.

This value carries such importance—and such relevance to our happiness. Children who learn to obey laws, to treat others fairly, and to be both repentant and forgiving can largely avoid the bitterness, the grudges, and the guilt along with the mental or physical imprisonment that are the consequences of not understanding or living the value of justice and mercy.

## GENERAL GUIDELINES

*Set up simple family laws.* This will help children know their limits and understand what is expected of them. It is best to do this in two "sessions." The first session is briefly to discuss with children the importance of laws. For example, there are government laws about stealing or cheating or hurting others. There are traffic laws that make it safer to be on the roads, and so on. We also need laws in our family so that we can be happier and so that everyone can know what is expected. Then ask the children for their input. What laws do they suggest? Make notes. Then tell them that you (as the parent or parents) will work on the laws and hold another family session when you are ready to discuss them.

After you (as parents) have decided on your family laws, write them on a chart and hold a second family session to explain them.

We suggest five simple, one-word laws that children can fully understand and easily remember:

- PEACE (no hitting, fighting, yelling, whining, etc.).
- PEGS (make a pegboard for each child, each with four pegs—one representing *family job,* one for *homework* and *practicing* (if the child is learning a musical instrument), and one for *evening things* (room clean, teeth brushed, in bed on time). The law is to get each peg in each day.
- ASKING (don't go anywhere, invite anyone over, etc., without permission).
- ORDER (room straight, pick up after self).
- OBEDIENCE (do what parents say).

Discuss how each law makes family members happier.

*Establish rewards to go with the keeping of each law and punishments to go with the breaking of each law.* This helps children learn cause and effect and understand elementary justice.

Enhance the "payday" system for pegs by having a bonus for each of the other laws they have done well on keeping during the week (peace, asking, order, obedience). Adjust the payday reward system to match the ages and needs of your children.

The main punishment for disobedience to the five family laws should be the *absence* of reward. On payday praise a child who did well and basically ignore (rather than chastise) a child who did poorly.

Certain laws also need specific punishments. These should be as close to "natural consequences" as possible. Some examples and suggestions:

- PEACE: As discussed earlier, have a "repenting bench" where children who argue or fight have to sit until they can tell you what *they* (not the *other* child) did wrong.
- ASKING: If a child does something or goes somewhere without permission, then the answer should be "no" next time to remind him.
- ORDER: Other family members pick up a child's things and throw them on his bed. He has to put them away that evening.
- OBEDIENCE: Establish the password of *please*. When you ask a child to do something, say *please*. His trigger response word is "Yes, Mother" or "Yes, Father." When a child doesn't obey, or forgets the response word, say, "Let's start over." Ask him

again, emphasizing *please*. If he still does not obey and say, "Yes, Mother," send him to his room.

*Add provisions for "repentance."* This is a good opportunity to teach children the powerful values (and skills) of asking for and giving forgiveness. Once family laws are established, along with rewards and punishments, add the principle of repentance. Teach small children that repentance consists of saying you're sorry for a specific thing, asking for forgiveness, and promising that you'll try never to do it again.

*Try* to use repentance rather than punishment wherever possible. Let children avoid sitting on the fighting bench if they repent to each other, or avoid going to their room if they say they are sorry for not obeying and quickly rectify the situation.

*Set the example.* Show that justice and mercy are *your* values and that you, too, are trying to learn to repent and forgive. When you make a mistake, lose your temper, fail to meet one of your responsibilities that involve a child, and so forth, make an obvious point of apologizing to the child and asking his forgiveness.

Strive to be viewed by your child not as one who is perfect but as one who is really trying to do better.

*Be fair and consistent, but also tender and merciful.* Again, teach this value by example. It is important to try to let neither rewardable behavior nor punishable behavior go unnoticed. Try to be consistent. On the other hand, don't make "quick justice" your whole goal. Always opt for repentance and forgiveness first, and only *resort* to punishment (showing your regret that it is necessary).

## Methods for Preschoolers

### Turn Taking

Begin to establish the idea of fairness. One of the first words that toddlers should learn is *turn*. Two-year-olds (and even pretwo's) can understand this most basic form of sharing. Help them to take a short turn with a toy and then say, "Jamie's turn," as they pass it to the other child. Then help them to watch and wait for a moment until it is their turn again.

Praise them generously every time they give a turn to the other child. As mentioned earlier, some sort of timing device makes "turns" work better. Use an oven clock or egg timer to help small children take turns of two or three minutes. Explain that equal time is fair.

### Add Friendliness to the Mix

Help your children see that they can have more fun and play *longer* with the toy they want if they learn to be *friendlier* and play together with it. As older preschoolers learn to share and take turns a little, you can explain to them that sometimes instead of taking individual turns with something, they can share by playing *together* with the same toy. Illustrate this to children in as many ways as you can think of. For example, in the case of a ball, each can bounce it and throw it individually, but both together could play catch! Or take a doll: Each could hold it and play independently, but both could play house as a fun game with the doll as the family baby.

## Simple Memorizing

This is a good way to help older preschoolers stay conscious of the sharing-caring-fairness mentality. If children do not understand the meaning of the word *rhyme,* explain it to them and illustrate it with nursery rhymes or simple poems. Then tell them that there are three words that rhyme with each other that help *everyone* to be happier. They are *fair, care,* and *share.* Talk about what each one means, and see if the child can remember all three.

Then, periodically, say to a child (especially when he needs it), "Can you remember the three rhyming words?"

## Discipline

Obedience and justice need to be closely related to how you discipline your children. Parents must make their own decisions about methods of discipline, but certain principles apply:

- Children should be disciplined in private rather than in public.
- Children will repeat the activities that attract the greatest attention. The key, therefore, is to give more attention for doing something right than for doing something wrong. Give lavish, open praise for the right and quiet, automatic discipline for the wrong.
- Children should know the reasons for the laws they are expected to keep and should think of obedience in terms of observing laws, not in terms of obeying people.

- Children find great security in consistent, predictable discipline.
- Discipline should be thought of as a way of teaching truth.
- Punishments should be administered only when laws are broken. When children make wrong decisions in areas not governed by law, their punishment should come through the natural consequences of those wrong choices. (If a child forgets his coat, he gets cold and needs no other punishment.)

## Methods for Elementary School Age

### Plant a Crop

Teach the law of the harvest. This will establish a metaphor and example with which you can reiterate principles of justice and cause and effect. Plant a small garden. If this is not possible, a single plant will do. Let a child be in charge of one particular crop or one particular plant. Teach him that with watering and weeding, the plant will grow tall and with neglect it will wilt, or be small, or die. Remind and assist, but let the initiative be with the child and let the law of the harvest and of cause and effect and of natural consequences take its course.

Then use the experience to show that there is a natural justice in the world and to explain other things. For example, if we're kind, others grow and give things to us. If we care for our things, they last longer. If we neglect things—or people—they don't do well and don't give us any return of joy or happiness.

### Add a Challenge to the Rhyming Words

Motivate and challenge your children to be fair with each other. Tell children that you have a challenge for them and that the challenge contains four words that rhyme: "I *dare* you to *share* and to *care* and be *fair*." Have them memorize the challenge. Tell them it is a hard challenge—harder by far (and much wiser) than some of the "dares" their friends might give them. Talk about what each word means. Give examples. Make it a catch-phrase in your conversations during this "month."

### The W.W.J.D. Award

Reward and praise children for fairness and for being forgiving—and to present the perfect example of both qualities. Add to your Sunday awards the W.W.J.D. ("What Would Jesus Do?") Award. (If you are non-Christian and feel better about some other identity, substitute another example of fairness and forgiveness.) As with each of the other awards, say, "Who's in the running for the W.W.J.D. Award?" Have children think through the week just past and call to mind any instance when they shared, let another child go first, took turns, and so on . . . *or* when they asked to be forgiven of something or forgave another person. Give the award accordingly.

Explain that the best way to earn this award or to keep it in mind is to be in the habit of asking yourself (several times a day), "What would Jesus do?"

### Sun and Cloud Game

This will help younger elementary-age children see that they can make themselves happy or miserable depending on their ability to repent and to forgive. Cut a yellow sun and a black cloud out of construction paper, along with two stick men or figures labeled "Billy" and "Eddy." Set Billy and Eddy on a table or on the floor and tell the following situations. Have the children put the sun over the head of the child who will be made happy by his actions and the cloud over the child whose actions will make him sad.

- A boy trips Eddy at school. Eddy is mad at the boy all day and keeps looking for a way to get even. (*Cloud.*)
- Billy opens his sister's drawer and takes some of her pencils. Then he feels badly about it and brings them back and says he is sorry. (*Sun.*)
- Eddy gets hit in the back by a ball another boy throws. It hurts for a minute and Eddy feels mad, but then he gets over it and tells the other boy he's okay and he knows the other boy didn't mean to do it. (*Sun.*)
- Billy leaves his mother's boots outside, and the dog chews one of them up. No one knows he was the one who left the boots out there, so he keeps it as a secret and doesn't repent or tell anyone. (*Cloud.*)
- And so on—make up your own.

### Comparison Story: The Smiths and the Joneses

This will help small children want to have family laws and want to live them.

Draw (or let the children draw) on a blackboard or large sheet of paper two houses, similar in size, next door to each other. Using the drawing as a visual aid, tell the following story in your own words.

"In this house (*point to one of the houses*) lived the Smith family. They had a boy and a girl named Steve and Sue. And they had *no* family laws. They didn't have to come to dinner at any certain time or go to bed at any certain time. They didn't have to put away their toys; they didn't have to mind their mother and father; they could watch television any time they wanted. (*Point to the other house.*) In this house lived the Jones family. They had a boy named Jimmy and a girl named Janie. They had family laws, and the children knew that they would be punished if they broke the laws.

"Now, let's pretend we can see right inside each of these houses and watch what is happening. Let's look into the Smiths' house first. Look at Steve and Sue's rooms. They look like pigpens. Nothing is ever put away; everything is on the floor. But where are Steve and Sue? Oh, there's Sue watching television. Her homework's not done. She'll be sorry tomorrow when her teacher asks her a question and she doesn't know the answer. There's Steve across the fence playing with a friend. His mom called him for dinner, but he didn't come. Now his food is cold and soggy. Look, his face is scratched from a fight with Sue over a toy. They don't even have laws against fighting.

"Let's look inside the Joneses' house. Jimmy's and Janie's clothes and toys are all neat and tidy, because their family has a law about that. Their family members are all sitting together having a nice dinner, because they have a law about that. Jimmy and Janie did their home-work before dinner, because they have a law for that too. When they've finished eating, they will be able to play and not worry about schoolwork that's not done."

Make your story personal by including things that are relevant to your family. Then involve the children in a discussion based on the following questions: Are laws good or bad? Do they make us happy or sad? Would we like to be like the Smiths? Should grown-ups have to obey laws too? What are some of our national laws? What are some of our community laws? What are some of our family laws? How does each make us happy?

### Role Reversal

This will help children see things from your perspective, and you from theirs.

When a serious disagreement arises concerning obedience in a particular matter, sit back for a moment, let things calm down, and then ask the child to pretend he's the mommy or daddy and you are the child. Set the stage for him. Tell him *why* he wants you, the child, to do (or not do) the particular thing. Then start the game.

Be a convincing "child." Play the role well and make your "parent" explain to you why he wants you to obey.

Some children role-play more naturally than others, but all children can learn the technique, and often it can be very helpful.

### Food Coloring in Water

One drop of food coloring can illustrate how holding one little grudge can make us miserable all over.

---

Our seven- and nine-year-old boys went through a little phase when they were fascinated with food coloring. They liked to make their milk blue and their eggs green. They also, unfortunately, experimented with coloring things other than food.

This fascination happened to come during the month we were trying to teach them the value of forgiveness and mercy. One of the boys had been carrying a grudge against a friend who had said something mean to him several weeks before.

I took a bottle of clear, clean water and told the boys that it represented their feelings and their joy in life. Then I put a single drop of red food coloring in the bottle and we watched the whole jar gradually turn pink. Then we talked about grudges and how one little one can make us feel bad all over. We talked about "poison" as another metaphor. Then we talked about forgiveness.

**—Richard**

---

## Methods for Adolescents

### "The Chronicles of Narnia"

Introduce your adolescents to perhaps the most remarkable youth-oriented literature ever written dealing with the subjects of justice and mercy. C. S. Lewis's seven-volume set, "The Chronicles of Narnia," teaches the principles of justice and mercy in a fantastically entertaining and clear manner. The first book in the series, *The Lion, the Witch and the Wardrobe,* is particularly appropriate to this topic. Twelve-year-olds and older are usually easily hooked once they start reading.

### Story: "Olga and the Rock"

Encourage adolescents to put things right in their lives rather than to let problems go and ignore them by telling the following story:

In the old country a woman named Olga had committed a serious sin. Her friend, Helga, a gossipy and self-righteous woman, told her she would have to go to the old sage who lived on the hill and ask him how to repent. Helga went along with her.

When they got to the sage's house, he listened to Olga's confession and told her to go into his garden and bring him the very large stone from the path. Olga obediently went out to do so. While she was gone, the old sage looked at Helga and said, "While we're waiting, will you please take this bag and gather all the small stones you can find and bring them here to me." Helga grumbled about it, but went ahead.

When both women returned—Olga, straining under the huge rock, and Helga with her bag of small stones—the sage said, "Now I will teach you of repentance. Olga, put the large stone back exactly where it was. Helga, put each of your small stones back exactly where it was—do not mix any of them up."

Discuss the story. Ask why little mistakes need to be corrected and "put right" as soon as possible.

While living in London, we took our adolescent children to the marvelous musical *Les Misérables,* based on Victor Hugo's classic novel. The story centers around the conflict between justice and mercy. Jean Valjean, a former prisoner and convict, is rehabilitated by the mercy and compassion of a priest. He becomes a great contributor, helper, and giver. Javert, his former jailer and later a policeman and magistrate, believes only in an ironclad, unforgiving form of justice and seeks to reimprison Jean Valjean on parole violations.

As we left the theater, we were glowing with the power and feeling of the music and the message. Then our thirteen-year-old said something that was worth more than any of it. He observed, "This is the first time I've ever understood how terrible laws and justice can be without any kind of forgiveness and mercy."

### Discussion: "Accepting Justice, Giving Mercy"

This will help older adolescents see the importance of both values and the relationship between the two. At an appropriate time ask older adolescents which they would rather receive—justice or mercy. Try to evolve this into a discussion where you are able to understand together that justice is something we should all be prepared to accept—for justice will always come, in some form, sooner or later. It is the law of the harvest and of cause and effect. Discuss the following quote by Emerson:

> Cause and effect are two sides of one fact. Every secret is told, every crime is punished. Every virtue is rewarded, every wrong is redressed, silence and certainty . . . cause and effect, means and ends, seed and fruit, cannot be severed; for the effect already blooms in the cause, the end pre-exists in the means, the fruit in the seed.

After discussing justice, turn to mercy. Explain that while we should *accept* justice, we should try to *give* mercy. Do not be interested in making others "pay" for their mistakes. Do not hold grudges or carry a chip on our shoulder. Discuss how these tendencies make us vindictive and vengeful and cause us to poison ourselves and our outlook.

### The Story of the Mote and the Beam

Remind adolescents that we are usually not in a position to judge others—and thus better off to try to understand and forgive rather than to condemn. Read or paraphrase the Bible story of the mote and the beam. (In brief: One person cannot remove a small speck or sliver from the eye of another person when there is a large sliver or beam in his own eye.) Also use the biblical admonition that only one without sin should throw the first stone (or condemn the sin of another). Tie this to the old phrase "People who live in glass houses should not throw rocks." Point out that since none of us is perfect, we should always be ready to understand and forgive imperfections in others.

# HOMEBASE

*An international organization of parents who share common concerns, ideas, and objectives as well as values. What the organization is and how to get involved . . .*

For more Americans than ever before, *parenting* has become a subject of deep interest, powerful concern, and enormous priority. The questions are not only how to raise children in a difficult world and what to teach them but how to balance the priority of children with the priorities of work and personal needs. More and more parents realize that parenting cannot be left to chance or to instinct . . . that success depends on clear goals, on well-thought-out approaches, and on a consistent stream of good input, information, and ideas.

Linda and Richard Eyre, perhaps more than any other American couple, have grappled with these challenges. As they have raised their own nine children, they have tried to better define the *process* of parenting and to become both a source and a forum for ideas that can help other parents around the world. *Teaching Your Children Values* is their fifth nationally published book on parenting and balance. They lecture widely, host a weekly national cable TV show called "Families Are Forever," and have addressed family topics on most regional and national TV talk shows, including "Donahue," "Sally Jessie Raphael," "Sonya Live," "Hour Magazine," and "The Home Show."

The Eyres' international co-op of parents, called HOMEBASE, publishes a monthly newsletter and distributes an in-home preschool program called *Teaching Children Joy,* a supplement for elementary education called *Teaching Children Responsibility,* a parents' program for dealing with adolescents called *Teaching Children Sensitivity,* and a time management program for stressed parents called *Lifebalance.* Please call (801) 581-0112 for further information.

# Index